Dr EH Baker PhD FRCP
Reader and Consultant in Clinical Pharmacology
Division of Basic Medical Sciences
St George's, University of London
London

Professor J Danesh MSc DPhil FRCP
Head, Department of Public Health and Primary Care
University of Cambridge
Cambridge

Dr JD Firth DM FRCP
Consultant Physician and Nephrologist
Addenbrooke's Hospital
Cambridge

Dr AD Hingorani FRCP
Senior Lecturer
Centre for Clinical Pharmacology and Therapeutics
University College London
London

Dr IS Mackenzie MBChB PhD MRCP(UK)
Clinical Lecturer
Clinical Pharmacology Unit
University of Cambridge
Cambridge

Dr R Sofat MRCP(UK)
Specialist Registrar
Centre for Clinical Pharmacology and Therapeutics
University College London
London

Dr HC Swannie MRCP(UK)
SpR Oncology
Mid Kent Oncology Centre
Maidstone Hospital
Kent

Professor CJM Whitty FRCP
Professor of International Health
Clinical Research Unit
London School of Hygiene and Tropical Medicine
London

Royal College
of Physicians
Setting higher medical standards

Published by:
Royal College of Physicians of London
11 St. Andrews Place
Regent's Park
London NW1 4LE
United Kingdom

Set and printed by Graphicraft Limited, Hong Kong

First edition published 2001
Reprinted 2004
Second edition published 2008

ISBN: 978-1-86016-265-7 (this book)
ISBN: 978-1-86016-260-2 (set)

Distribution Information:
Jerwood Medical Education Resource Centre
Royal College of Physicians of London
11 St. Andrews Place
Regent's Park
London NW1 4LE
United Kingdom
Tel: +44 (0)207 935 1174 ext 422/490
Fax: +44 (0)207 486 6653
Email: merc@rcplondon.ac.uk
Web: http://www.rcplondon.ac.uk/

MEDICAL MASTERCLASS

EDITOR-IN-CHIEF

JOHN D FIRTH DM FRCP

Consultant Physician and Nephrologist
Addenbrooke's Hospital
Cambridge

SCIENTIFIC BACKGROUND TO MEDICINE 2

EDITORS

JOHN D FIRTH DM FRCP

Consultant Physician and Nephrologist
Addenbrooke's Hospital
Cambridge

EMMA H BAKER PhD FRCP

Reader and Consultant in Clinical Pharmacology
St George's, University of London
London

Second Edition

Royal College
of Physicians
Setting higher medical standards

Disclaimer

Although every effort has been made to ensure that drug doses and other information are presented accurately in this publication, the ultimate responsibility rests with the prescribing physician. Neither the publishers nor the authors can be held responsible for any consequences arising from the use of information contained herein. Any product mentioned in this publication should be used in accordance with the prescribing information prepared by the manufacturers.

The information presented in this publication reflects the opinions of its contributors and should not be taken to represent the policy and views of the Royal College of Physicians of London, unless this is specifically stated.

Every effort has been made by the contributors to contact holders of copyright to obtain permission to reproduce copyrighted material. However, if any have been inadvertently overlooked, the publisher will be pleased to make the necessary arrangements at the first opportunity.

CONTENTS

FOREWORD

Since its initial publication in 2001, *Medical Masterclass* has been regarded as a key learning and teaching resource for physicians around the world. The resource was produced in part to meet the vision of the Royal College of Physicians: *'Doctors of the highest quality, serving patients well'*. This vision continues and, along with advances in clinical practice and changes in the format of the MRCP(UK) exam, has justified the publication of this second edition.

The MRCP(UK) is an international examination that seeks to advance the learning of and enhance the training process for physicians worldwide. On passing the exam physicians are recognised as having attained the required knowledge, skills and manner appropriate for training at a specialist level. However, passing the exam is a challenge. The pass rate at each sitting of the written papers is about 40%. Even the most prominent consultants have had to sit each part of the exam more than once in order to pass. With this challenge in mind, the College has produced *Medical Masterclass*, a comprehensive learning resource to help candidates with the preparation that is key to making the grade.

Medical Masterclass has been produced by the Education Department of the College. A work of this size represents a formidable amount of effort by the Editor-in-Chief – Dr John Firth – and his team of editors and authors. I would like to thank our colleagues for this wonderful educational product and wholeheartedly recommend it as an invaluable learning resource for all physicians preparing for their MRCP(UK) examination.

Professor Ian Gilmore MD PRCP
President of the Royal College of Physicians

PREFACE

The second edition of *Medical Masterclass* is produced and published by the Education Department of the Royal College of Physicians of London. It comprises 12 textbooks, a companion interactive website and two CD-ROMs. Its aim is to help doctors in their first few years of training to improve their medical knowledge and skills; and in particular to (a) learn how to deal with patients who are acutely ill, and (b) pass postgraduate examinations, such as the MRCP(UK) or European Diploma in Internal Medicine.

The 12 textbooks are divided as follows: two cover the scientific background to medicine, one is devoted to general clinical skills [including specific guidance on exam technique for PACES, the practical assessment of clinical examination skills that is the final part of the MRCP(UK) exam], one deals with acute medicine and the other eight cover the range of medical specialties.

The core material of each of the medical specialties is dealt with in seven sections:

- Case histories – you are presented with letters of referral commonly received in each specialty and led through the ways in which the patients' histories should be explored, and what should then follow in the way of investigation and/or treatment.

- Physical examination scenarios – these emphasise the logical analysis of physical signs and sensible clinical reasoning: 'having found this, what would you do?'

- Communication and ethical scenarios – what are the difficult issues that commonly arise in each specialty? What do you actually say to the 'frequently asked (but still very difficult) questions?'

- Acute presentations – what are the priorities if you are the doctor seeing the patient in the Emergency Department or the Medical Admissions Unit?

- Diseases and treatments – structured concise notes.

- Investigations and practical procedures – more short and to-the-point notes.

- Self assessment questions – in the form used in the MRCP(UK) Part 1 and Part 2 exams.

The companion website – which is continually updated – enables you to take mock MRCP(UK) Part 1 or Part 2 exams, or to be selective in the questions you tackle (if you want to do ten questions on cardiology, or any other specialty, you can do). For every question you complete you can see how your score compares with that of others who have logged onto the site and attempted it. The two CD-ROMs each contain 30 interactive cases requiring diagnosis and treatment.

I hope that you enjoy using *Medical Masterclass* to learn more about medicine, which – whatever is happening politically to primary care, hospitals and medical career structures – remains a wonderful occupation. It is sometimes intellectually and/or emotionally very challenging, and also sometimes extremely rewarding, particularly when reduced to the essential of a doctor trying to provide best care for a patient.

John Firth DM FRCP
Editor-in-Chief

ACKNOWLEDGEMENTS

Medical Masterclass has been produced by a team. The names of those who have written or edited material are clearly indicated elsewhere, but without the support of many other people it would not exist. Naming names is risky, but those worthy of particular note include: Sir Richard Thompson (College Treasurer) and Mrs Winnie Wade (Director of Education), who steered the project through committees that are traditionally described as labyrinthine, and which certainly seem so to me; and also Arthur Wadsworth (Project Co-ordinator) and Don Liu in the College Education Department office. Don is a veteran of the first edition of *Medical Masterclass*, and it would be fair to say that without his great efforts a second edition might not have seen the light of day.

John Firth DM FRCP
Editor-in-Chief

We have created a range of icon boxes that sit among the text of the various *Medical Masterclass* modules. They are there to help you identify key information and to make learning easier and more enjoyable. Here is a brief explanation:

> Iron-deficiency anaemia with a change in bowel habit in a middle-aged or older patient means colonic malignancy until proved otherwise.

This icon is used to highlight points of particular importance.

> Dietary deficiency is very rarely, if ever, the sole cause of iron-deficiency anaemia.

This icon is used to indicate common or important drug interactions, pitfalls of practical procedures, or when to take symptoms or signs particularly seriously.

> A man with a renal transplant is immunosuppressed with ciclosporin, azathioprine and prednisolone. He develops recurrent gout and is started on allopurinol. Four weeks later he is admitted with septicaemia and found to be profoundly leucopenic. The problem is that allopurinol, by inhibiting xanthine oxidase, has inhibited the metabolism of azathioprine, rendering a 'normal dose' toxic.

Case examples/case histories are used to demonstrate why and how an understanding of the scientific background to medicine helps in the practice of clinical medicine.

CLINICAL PHARMACOLOGY

Authors:

EH Baker, AD Hingorani, IS Mackenzie, R Sofat and HC Swannie

Editor:

EH Baker

Editor-in-Chief:

JD Firth

'The desire to take medicine is perhaps the greatest feature which distinguishes man from animal.' (Sir William Osler)

For most doctors the major intervention open to them in treating their patients is drug therapy, which can alleviate symptoms, reverse pathology, modify risk and even improve survival. However, not all effects of drugs are advantageous: every prescriber must weigh the risks and benefits of prescribing, and have a sound understanding of the ways in which drugs cause adverse effects and of those circumstances where prescribing carries enhanced risks. The art of good prescribing is in knowing how to apply the best available evidence to each individual patient in order to achieve the maximum benefit with the minimum of risk.

 Example 1: Individualising therapy

A 54-year-old man presents to his GP with exertional chest pain, typical of angina. He has type 2 diabetes mellitus (diet controlled) and is hypertensive. His current medications are ramipril 7.5 mg once a day, salbutamol MDI prn and simvastatin 20 mg nocte. On examination mild wheeze can be heard throughout the chest. His ankles are swollen. While arranging investigations to confirm the diagnosis and determine further management, the doctor wishes to start treatment to relieve the patient's symptoms. He considers antianginal medications such as beta-blockers, calcium channel antagonists and nitrates. It is important to ask the following.

- What is the evidence for efficacy of each of the drugs and what are the potential risks?
- Which choice is the best in terms of risk–benefit analysis?

Clinical approach

The aim of drug therapy in this situation should be to relieve symptoms and to reduce the risk of future cardiovascular disease events, while minimising the adverse effects of what will be long-term drug therapy. In Europe 67% of patients with angina are treated first with a beta-blocker and 27% with a calcium channel antagonist. Points to consider when making the decision include the following.

- Both beta-blockers and calcium channel antagonists have been shown to be effective in relieving symptoms in chronic stable angina, although beta-blockers may reduce the frequency of episodes compared with calcium channel antagonists [odds ratio (OR) 0.31, 95% confidence interval (CI) 0.00–0.62; $P = 0.05$].
- The rate of cardiac death and myocardial infarction (MI) has not been shown to be signficantly different (OR 0.97, 95% CI 0.67–1.38; $P = 0.79$) between beta-blockers and calcium channel antagonists. However, beta-blockers are associated with improved outcomes in patients with left ventricular dysfunction and after MI.
- Beta-blockers are associated with decreased insulin sensitivity, exercise capacity and sexual function, increased weight and fatigue, and they may also precipitate bronchospasm.
- This patient has type 2 diabetes, is a relatively young man and the prescription of salbutamol and examination findings should alert you to the possibility of asthma.
- Calcium channel antagonists have been shown to reduce the need for angiography in patients with angina, suggesting symptomatic benefit. However, their beneficial effects on mortality and MI may relate to their antihypertensive rather than their antianginal effect.
- Calcium channel antagonists are relatively negatively inotropic and can cause ankle oedema, which may be unacceptable in a patient who already has swollen ankles.
- Despite their frequent prescription, there are minimal data comparing long-acting nitrates with beta-blockers and calcium channel antagonists.
- Review of the patient's current prescriptions reveals that he is already taking an angiotensin-converting enzyme inhibitor, which has preventive value in coronary artery disease, and the doctor will also want to consider antiplatelet therapy with aspirin after an assessment of the risks of gastrointestinal adverse effects.

FURTHER READING

Heidenreich PA, McDonald KM, Hastie T, *et al*. Meta-analysis of trials comparing beta-blockers, calcium antagonists, and nitrates for stable angina. *JAMA* 1999; 281: 1927–36.

Lubsen J, Wagener G, Kirwan BA, *et al*. Effect of long-acting nifedipine on mortality and cardiovascular morbidity in patients with symptomatic stable angina and hypertension: the ACTION trial. *J. Hypertens*. 2005; 23: 641–8.

Opie LH, Commerford PJ and Gersh BJ. Controversies in stable coronary artery disease. *Lancet* 2006; 367: 69–78.

Yusuf S, Sleight P, Pogue J, *et al*. Effects of an angiotensin-converting-enzyme inhibitor, ramipril, on cardiovascular events in high-risk patients. The Heart Outcomes Prevention Evaluation Study Investigators. *N. Engl. J. Med*. 2000; 342: 145–53.

administered, will it interact with other substances, what are the side effects and what is the likely benefit that might reasonably be expected from using a particular drug in this particular patient? What is the cost of the drug, does the risk–benefit seem favourable and what does the patient think?

Safe and rational prescribers will address all these questions whenever they prescribe. Even in familiar circumstances where they might feel entirely confident, a critical analysis of the decision to prescribe will benefit and protect patients.

1.1 Risks versus benefits

'One of the first duties of the physician is to educate the masses not to take medicine.' (Sir William Osler)

Is drug treatment appropriate? Are other interventions known to be as, or even more, effective? Is prescription for lipid-lowering therapy necessary? Has the patient received appropriate advice about lifestyle modification? When are antibiotics appropriate?

If prescription is appropriate, which class of drugs would be most appropriate for an individual patient, and from within a seemingly homogeneous class of drugs, which individual product should be chosen? At what dosage should the chosen drug be used, by which route, in what formulation and for how long? When should it be

Example 2: Should you risk harm while trying to do good?

An 87-year-old woman is admitted after a series of falls that are thought to be related to her poor visual acuity and advanced osteoarthritis. She is found to have mild heart failure with mitral regurgitation and atrial fibrillation, and the question is raised of whether she should receive anticoagulation with warfarin to protect against emboli. What are the likely risks and benefits of this and how would you make your decision?

Clinical approach

The combination of atrial fibrillation, heart failure and mitral regurgitation places this woman at high risk of stroke and there is good evidence that adjusted-dose warfarin provides the best risk reduction in this circumstance. However, in view of her impaired visual acuity and propensity to falls, what do you think the risks are for this particular patient and how do they match up against any theoretical benefit? In this circumstance, the risks probably outweigh the benefits.

1.2 Safe prescribing

'There are no really "safe" biologically active drugs, there are only "safe" physicians.' (Harold A. Kaminetzky)

Safe prescribing requires knowledge and understanding of the interaction between an individual drug and an individual patient. Pharmacokinetics (the way in which the body handles a drug) and pharmacodynamics (the way a drug affects the body) are essential to understanding and predicting this interaction. Both may be affected by drug- or patient-specific factors. For instance, is a drug highly lipid soluble and therefore likely to be well absorbed when given orally? Does it have a short half-life and require very frequent dosing? Does the patient have impaired hepatic or renal function that will affect the metabolism and clearance of the drug? Is the patient at the extremes of age or is she pregnant? What other drugs (prescribed or not) is the patient taking? Are there any clinically significant interactions that could result? Is there a risk of accidental (or deliberate) overdose?

Drug interactions can kill: a cautionary tale

A 79-year-old woman with atrial fibrillation developed a second episode of moderately severe depression and her psychiatrist prescribed a selective serotonin reuptake inhibitor (SSRI) which had helped her before. He had extensive experience in prescribing SSRIs but was unaware of a potentially significant interaction between the SSRI and the warfarin that she was taking, and did not think to check the *British National Formulary* (*BNF*) for interactions. The patient became over-anticoagulated, bled into her retroperitoneum and subsequently died. Had he checked the appendix in the *BNF* for interactions, the INR could have been closely monitored, the dosage of warfarin adjusted as necessary, and the bleed and the patient's subsequent death avoided.

Specific knowledge will be required of drug interactions involving the common metabolic pathways (eg cytochrome P450) and of the indications for therapeutic monitoring of drug levels. Prescribing in patients with renal or liver disease, in pregnancy, or in those with a history of drug allergy or genetic susceptibility to adverse drug effects will demand special consideration.

Alongside such knowledge, a safe prescriber will also know how to access up-to-date information about drugs (eg from the *BNF*, local formularies, pharmacists and online resources). There is an ever-expanding literature on the efficacy and safety of existing drugs, and every year around 30–40 new drugs are licensed in the UK. All prescribers must know where to find authoritative advice and guidance. They will be skilled in obtaining an accurate drug history and in writing clear and unambiguous prescriptions. They will understand the importance of a patient participating in the decision to undertake drug treatment (patient concordance) and the effect this has on adherence to therapy. They will be able to explain clearly to patients the reasons for taking a particular drug, what the benefit to them might be, what they can reasonably expect and what to be aware of in terms of side effects.

Develop the habit of routinely referring to the *BNF* for all but the most familiar prescribing decisions.

1.3 Rational prescribing

Example 3: Which analgesic?

A patient has an inguinal hernia repair as a day case and at home that night develops pain of moderate severity. He has a choice of analgesic at home: paracetamol 1.0 g, ibuprofen 400 mg or codeine 60 mg. Which drug should he take (assuming that he can have only one) to maximise his chances of gaining an analgesic effect? (See *Pain Relief and Palliative Care*, Sections 1.1.1, 1.3.1 and 2.1.)

Clinical approach

When presented with this question I suspect that most doctors would rate these drugs in descending order of effectiveness as follows: codeine, ibuprofen, paracetamol. However, a careful meta-analysis of randomised controlled trials in acute pain has clearly shown that the rank order is ibuprofen 400 mg with a number needed to treat (NNT) of 3 (see *Statistics, Epidemiology, Clinical Trials and Meta-Analyses*, Clinical Trials and Meta-Analyses), followed by paracetamol 1.0 g (NNT = 4.6), with codeine 60 mg coming in a poor last with an NNT of 16. Preconceptions and medical mythology are hard to shift!

A rational prescriber should understand the process by which drugs become available through a series of preclinical and clinical trials. He or she will then be able to evaluate and interpret the evidence available for the efficacy and safety of a particular drug for a particular

condition and apply this to the patient in front of them. Does the trial data apply to the individual patient under consideration? What other sources of evidence are available on which to base prescribing decisions? Clinical guidelines, local formularies and peer-reviewed publications are all resources for evidence-based prescribing.

The responsible and rational prescriber should also not be afraid to consider the cost of drugs when prescribing. The most expensive drug is not necessarily the best, and the competing interests of manufacturers, purchasers, prescribers and patients, often played out in the full glare of media publicity, do not always serve to clarify the issues surrounding individual prescribing decisions. Drugs are big business: the National Health Service spends around 10% of its annual budget on drugs (about £8 billion) and prescribers should always be aware of the potential for conflicts of interest that arise.

1.4 The role of clinical pharmacology

Management of the adverse effects of drugs, allergy, drug reactions, poisoning, overdose, and illicit drug use will always be an important part of the work of a physician. At least 5% of acute admissions to hospital are directly attributable to adverse effects of drugs (not including where drugs have been used for deliberate self-harm) and up to 20% of hospital inpatients suffer significant drug-related illness. Knowledge of the features of poisoning with specific drugs and skills in assessing the severity of overdose and poisoning are essential (see *Acute Medicine*, Section 2.1.2).

Clinical pharmacologists specialise in the scientific basis of therapeutics (outlined in this section), in the development and critical evaluation of drugs, and in the management of drug-related clinical problems. They are actively involved in the monitoring and management of the use of medicines and in the development of evidence-based guidelines for their use. These activities underpin both safe and rational prescribing in general, and provide the basis for the use of drugs as discussed in each of the *Medical Masterclass* modules.

The format of this section of *Medical Masterclass* differs from the other clinical sections in not being organised on the basis of individual case scenarios, although many common clinical examples are used to illustrate its themes. However, the principles and practice of clinical pharmacology underlie all the clinical scenarios, as well as the diseases and treatments discussed in the other sections. The section should be read alongside the Foundation Programme syllabus in

clinical pharmacology (Academy of Medical Royal Colleges, Curriculum for the Foundation Years in Postgraduate Education and Training: available at http://www.mmc.nhs.uk/download/Curriculum-for-the-foundation-years-in-postgraduate-education-and-training.pdf) and the following issues considered.

- Effects of disease on prescribing: hepatic, renal.

- Effects of patient factors on prescribing: age (ie children and the elderly), drug allergy, genetic susceptibility to adverse drug reactions, pregnancy, cultural/religious belief.

- Effects of drug interactions.

- Metabolism by cytochrome P450 isoenzymes.

- Drugs that require therapeutic monitoring.

- Common drug error situations.

- Evidence-based and safe prescribing using National Institute for Health and Clinical Excellence (NICE) or Scottish Intercollegiate Guidelines Network (SIGN) guidelines.

- Principles of safe prescribing of oxygen and blood products.

- Factors that affect concordance.

- Principles of safe prescribing for children and older people.

FURTHER READING

Bennett PN and Brown MJ. *Clinical Pharmacology*, 9th edn. Edinburgh: Churchill Livingstone, 2003.

Brunton L, Lazo J and Parker K. *Goodman & Gilman's the Pharmacological Basis of Therapeutics*, 11th edn. New York: McGraw-Hill, 2005.

Grahame-Smith DG and Aronson AK. *Oxford Textbook of Clinical Pharmacology and Drug Therapy*, 3rd edn. Oxford: Oxford University Press, 2002.

McQuay HJ and Moore RA. *An Evidence-based Resource for Pain Relief*. Oxford: Oxford University Press, 1998.

Reid JL, Rubin P and Walters M. *Lecture Notes: Clinical Pharmacology and Therapeutics*, 7th edn. Oxford: Blackwell Science, 2006.

2.1 Introduction

The word 'pharmacokinetics' comes from the Greek (*pharmakon*, drug; *kineein*, to move). It literally describes the ways in which drugs move into, out of and around the body, and how they are handled by its tissues and organs. We use pharmacokinetics, either consciously or subconsciously, every time a prescribing decision is made, eg when considering how much and how often to give a drug, by what route to administer the drug and when informing the patient how quickly it may work. Understanding pharmacokinetics is therefore of great importance in daily clinical practice. In this section, examples of clinical problems are described and the pharmacokinetic principles required to solve these problems discussed.

2.2 Drug absorption

Example 4: Diarrhoea and the pill

A 24-year-old woman has been in hospital for 5 days with severe diarrhoea. During admission she has been taking her regular oral contraceptive pill. On discharge she asks for information about her risk of becoming pregnant.

Clinical approach

Your main concern is that her severe diarrhoea has impaired absorption of the oral contraceptive across the gastrointestinal tract, reducing plasma levels of oestrogen and progesterone and thereby increasing her chances of contraceptive failure.

Pharmacokinetics of gastrointestinal absorption

Most drug absorption in the gastrointestinal tract occurs by diffusion. For diffusion to occur the drug must be dissolved so that individual drug molecules come into contact with the gut epithelium, and

it must be chemically lipid soluble so that it can cross cell membranes (Fig. 1 and Table 1). Diffusion is greatest where the following conditions are present.

- A large surface area for absorption: most drug absorption occurs in the small intestine.

- A large concentration gradient driving drug absorption from the gut lumen to the interstitium: this is increased by larger drug doses, which increase luminal concentration, or greater intestinal blood flow, which lowers interstitial drug concentration by removing the absorbed drug.

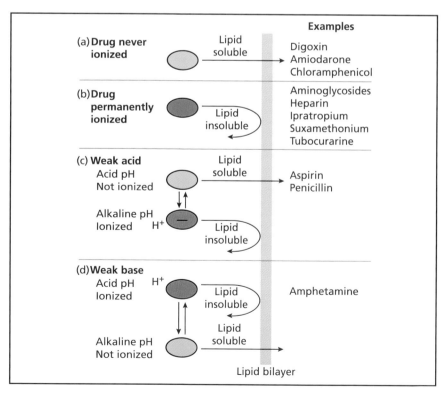

▲ **Fig. 1** The chemical properties of a drug affect its ability to cross cell membranes. (**a**) Drugs that are not ionised (non-polar) are lipid soluble and can cross cell membranes. (**b**) Ionised drugs are lipid insoluble and cannot cross cell membranes. (**c, d**) Many drugs are weak acids or weak bases; their lipid solubility and ability to cross cell membranes depend on the environment's pH.

TABLE 1 GENERAL PHARMACOKINETIC PROPERTIES OF LIPID-SOLUBLE AND LIPID-INSOLUBLE DRUGS

	Lipid soluble	Lipid insoluble
Gastrointestinal absorption	Good	Poor
Administration	Can be given orally	May need to be given parenterally
Distribution	Wide, including across the blood–brain barrier and placenta	Limited, may not penetrate the blood–brain barrier or cross the placenta
Metabolism and elimination	Metabolism required to decrease lipid solubility before elimination	May be eliminated without metabolism
Plasma half-life	May be prolonged by a 'reservoir' of drug in tissues and by requirement for metabolism	Often short, as elimination does not require metabolism

Other factors that affect intestinal drug absorption are shown in Table 2.

TABLE 2 FACTORS THAT DETERMINE DRUG ABSORPTION ACROSS THE GASTROINTESTINAL (GI) TRACT

Properties of drug	Properties of GI tract	Interaction between drug and GI tract
Physical preparation Chemical properties Dose	Site of absorption Surface area Intestinal transit time: decreased (faster) by infection, increased (slower) by food Blood supply Enterohepatic circulation	Interaction with food or other drugs in gut lumen: • Calcium, aluminium or magnesium in milk or antacids reduce tetracycline absorption • Activated charcoal reduces absorption of drugs taken in overdose • Cholestyramine interferes with absorption of warfarin, digoxin and thyroxine Ingested drug altered by pH or enzymes in gut lumen, eg benzylpenicillin destroyed by gastric acid, insulin digested by gut enzymes

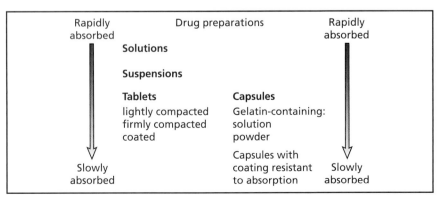

▲ Fig. 2 Rates of absorption of oral pharmaceutical preparations.

of drugs to control absorption characteristics (Fig. 2), eg nifedipine is available in a number of different preparations that are absorbed at different rates. Nifedipine capsules contain liquid that is absorbed immediately, causing a rapid rise in plasma drug concentration (Fig. 3) and rapid onset of effect: these are rarely used now because they lower blood pressure too quickly, which may precipitate a stroke. Nifedipine is also formulated as slow-release tablets (nifedipine SR) and as long-acting tablets with an absorption-resistant coating (nifedipine LA). The slower absorption of drug from these tablets results in slower elevation in plasma drug concentrations (Fig. 3) and a more controlled and safer onset of blood pressure lowering effect. Additionally, plasma drug levels are sustained for longer, prolonging the duration of action of the drug.

Other drug preparations are designed to release the drug at a specific site in the gastrointestinal tract where its actions are required, eg sulfasalazine, which is used to maintain remission in ulcerative colitis, consists of sulfapyridine and 5-aminosalicylic acid joined by an azo bond. This complex passes unchanged through the gastrointestinal tract until it reaches the large intestine, where colonic bacteria split the azo bond and release the 5-aminosalicylic acid to act on the colon.

Drug preparations and absorption

Drug manufacturers alter the physical and chemical properties

Example 4: Diarrhoea and the pill (*continued*)

Clinical approach

Severe diarrhoea causes decreased intestinal transit time (transit is faster). In our patient on the oral contraceptive pill, this would have reduced contact of ingested hormones

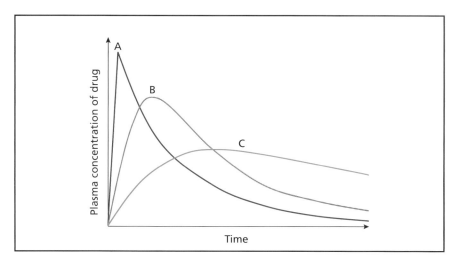

▲ **Fig. 3** Graph of plasma concentration of drug against time. When drugs are given by intravenous injection (A), they reach maximum concentration in the plasma almost immediately. The plasma concentration subsequently falls due to drug distribution, metabolism and elimination (see Section 2.6). When drugs are given orally (B, C), the plasma concentration continues to rise until the amount of drug absorbed equals the amount being distributed, metabolised and eliminated from the body. Drug B is rapidly absorbed, reaches maximum plasma concentration and is effective rapidly, but has a short duration of action. Drug C is more slowly absorbed and has a flatter time–concentration profile, characteristics that will give a more even drug response and longer duration of action.

- digoxin;

- morphine;

- chloramphenicol;

- vecuronium (muscle relaxant);

- rifampicin.

Routes of drug administration

In general, the oral route is used for drug administration because it is acceptable and convenient for the patient. However, other routes of administration (Table 3) may be necessary or preferable for drugs that:

- are not absorbed when given orally;

- are an irritant to the gastrointestinal tract;

- cause side effects when given orally, which can be avoided by topical administration;

with the intestinal epithelium and thus reduced the absorption of oestrogen and progesterone. Severe diarrhoea may also disrupt the enterohepatic circulation, which maintains plasma concentrations of ethinylestradiol (Fig. 4). A fall in the plasma levels of oestrogen and progesterone increases the chance of ovulation and conception. Armed with this pharmacokinetic knowledge you should advise your patient as follows.

- To continue the oral contraceptive pill, but use other contraceptive methods until she is well, and for 7 days after recovery.
- That the diarrhoea is more likely to have reduced her contraceptive protection if she is at the beginning or end of her pill cycle. At these times, reduced hormone absorption will extend the duration of low plasma hormone levels and protection against pregnancy is reduced. She should therefore omit the 7-day pill-free interval if she is at the end of a cycle.

- ethinylestradiol (in many oral contraceptives);

- sulindac (NSAID);

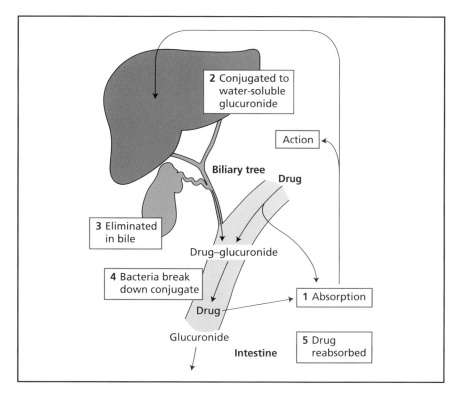

▲ **Fig. 4** The enterohepatic circulation. Absorbed drugs (step 1) are modified by conjugation, eg with glucuronate, to increase water solubility (step 2) and are excreted in the bile (step 3). Once in the gut, bacteria act to break up the drug–glucuronide conjugate (step 4). If the released unconjugated drug is lipid soluble, it will be reabsorbed in the intestine (step 5). This 'enterohepatic circulation' of drugs can form a circulating reservoir of up to 20% of the total concentration of a drug in the body. The enterohepatic circulation is interrupted by antibiotics that alter gut flora (eg neomycin) and less so by severe diarrhoea.

The following drugs are recycled by the enterohepatic circulation (Fig. 4) and their effects can be seriously compromised if this is disrupted:

TABLE 3 ALTERNATIVE ROUTES OF DRUG ADMINISTRATION: THEIR USES AND PROBLEMS

	Route	Use	Potential problems
GI tract	Buccal Sublingual Rectal	Drugs requiring quick action, eg buccal aspirin during MI and sublingual glyceryl trinitrate for angina Where drugs cannot be swallowed but do not need to be injected, eg sublingual buprenorphine analgesia or rectal metronidazole after GI surgery	Many drugs are not absorbed sufficiently by these routes Rectal administration may be unacceptable to patient
Injection (parenteral)	Intravenous Intramuscular Subcutaneous Intradermal Into body cavity or tissue	Where drugs cannot be absorbed or are destroyed in the GI tract (see Table 1) Where swift onset or termination of drug action is required	Injection may be painful and unacceptable to patient Requires help or training by a healthcare professional May introduce infection
Topical	ENT Eye Skin Inhaled	For local use: administered directly to site of action and reduces systemic side effects of the drug, eg inhaled vs oral steroids for asthma For systemic use: alternative routes that avoid injections where GI administration is not possible, eg intranasal vasopressin	May get local allergy Despite local administration systemic effects may occur, eg side effects of beta-blockers given into eye for glaucoma

ENT, ear, nose and throat; GI, gastrointestinal; MI, myocardial infarction.

- act too slowly or unpredictably when given orally;

- undergo extensive (Table 4) or unpredictable presystemic metabolism.

Non-oral routes of drug administration and some of their advantages and disadvantages are shown in Table 3.

Drug availability

A drug exerts its action once it has reached the circulation and gained access to tissues and receptors. Drugs injected directly into a vein are 100% available. Drugs given orally are less than 100% available because the drug may be incompletely absorbed or it may undergo presystemic metabolism by drug-metabolising enzymes in the gut wall, portal circulation or liver before reaching the systemic circulation. Food affects the availability of drugs taken orally in a variety of ways. If drugs are poorly absorbed because they are sparingly lipid soluble (eg atenolol), food reduces absorption and availability. In contrast, food increases the availability of drugs that undergo extensive presystemic drug metabolism because it increases the portal flow and rate of drug presentation to the liver by saturating and bypassing metabolic pathways. A glass of grapefruit juice or fresh grapefruit segments irreversibly inhibits drug-metabolising enzymes in the intestinal wall, thereby increasing the absorption and availability of a whole range of drugs including ciclosporin, statins, calcium channel blockers and antiarrhythmics.

Where a drug undergoes extensive presystemic metabolism, the intravenous dose required to achieve a given plasma level and have a therapeutic effect is lower than the oral dose required to have the same effect (Table 4). It is particularly important to check the dose of drugs that can be given both orally and intravenously before administration by either route.

FURTHER READING

Begg EJ. *Instant Clinical Pharmacology*. Oxford: Blackwell Publishing, 2003.

Tozer TN and Rowland M. *Introduction to Pharmacokinetics and Pharmacodynamics: The Quantitative Basis of Drug Therapy*. Baltimore: Lippincott, Williams and Wilkins, 2006.

TABLE 4 EXAMPLE OF ORAL AND PARENTERAL DOSES OF DRUGS UNDERGOING EXTENSIVE PRESYSTEMIC (FIRST-PASS) METABOLISM

Drug undergoing extensive presystemic metabolism	Oral dose (mg)	Comparable intravenous dose
Metoprolol	50–100	5–15 mg
Atenolol	50–100	2.5–10 mg
Verapamil	40–120	5–10 mg
Salbutamol	4	250 µg

2.3 Drug distribution

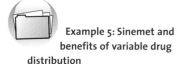

Example 5: Sinemet and benefits of variable drug distribution

A 73-year-old man with Parkinson's disease is commenced on Sinemet (levodopa with carbidopa). After 1 week he is considerably more mobile, but has developed nausea and vomiting. (See *Neurology*, Section 2.3.1.)

Clinical approach

Loss of dopaminergic neurons in the extrapyramidal system results in abnormal movement control with hypokinesia, rigidity and tremor, the symptoms of Parkinson's disease. These symptoms can be relieved by giving levodopa, which is converted by dopa decarboxylase to dopamine in the brain. However, levodopa is also metabolised by dopa decarboxylase to dopamine in the periphery, where it causes side effects. Co-administration of carbidopa (a dopa decarboxylase inhibitor) prevents peripheral levodopa metabolism and side effects. However, as it does not cross the blood–brain barrier, carbidopa does not prevent the central conversion of levodopa to dopamine. The success of Sinemet for Parkinson's disease is therefore dependent on the different distribution properties of the drugs that are used.

The side effects of nausea and vomiting seen in this patient are caused by the action of dopamine at the chemoreceptor trigger zone for emesis in the brainstem (area postrema). This area has a deficient blood–brain barrier, hence carbidopa reduces the incidence of nausea and vomiting in patients receiving levodopa from 80% to 15%.

Pharmacokinetics of drug distribution

Distribution of individual drugs into different body compartments depends on (Fig. 5):

- lipid solubility of the drug;

- binding of the drug to plasma and tissue proteins.

Lipid solubility and drug distribution

Lipid-insoluble drugs remain largely in the extracellular water. Lipid-soluble drugs distribute freely throughout the body and cross into transcellular compartments such as the cerebrospinal fluid (CSF). Many lipid-soluble drugs are stored in physical solution in fat (see Fig. 1 and Table 1).

The lipid solubility of drugs that are weak acids or weak bases will change depending on the pH of the body compartment that they occupy, eg a weak acid such as aspirin (salicylic acid) will be un-ionised and lipid soluble at low pH in the stomach and hence freely absorbed. However, once in intestinal cells that have an intracellular pH of 7.35–7.45, the salicylic acid becomes ionised and is less able to move out of the cell. This process is known as pH partitioning.

Plasma protein and tissue binding

Some drugs bind extensively to plasma proteins and so remain largely in the plasma. Other drugs are extensively bound to tissue sites, usually proteins, phospholipids or

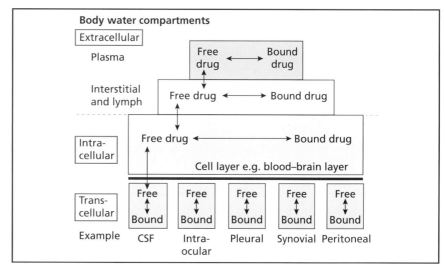

▲ **Fig. 5** Distribution of drugs in the body. Lipid-insoluble drugs remain in the extracellular water because they cannot cross cell membranes. Lipid-soluble drugs may cross freely into all body water compartments. Drugs that are extensively bound to plasma proteins stay mostly in the plasma, even if lipid soluble. Tissue-bound drugs form a drug reservoir in the tissues. CSF, cerebrospinal fluid.

TABLE 5 EXAMPLES OF DRUGS WHICH BIND TO PLASMA AND TISSUE PROTEINS OR FORM A RESERVOIR IN LIPIDS

Reservoir site	Drug
Plasma proteins	
Albumin	Acidic drugs, eg warfarin, diazepam, furosemide, clofibrate, phenytoin, amitriptyline
Lipoprotein, α-acid glycoprotein	Basic drugs, eg quinidine, chlorpromazine, imipramine
Other sites	
Tissue sites	Amiodarone, chloroquine, digoxin
Lipid stores	Benzodiazepines, verapamil, lidocaine

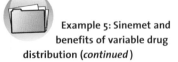

Example 5: Sinemet and benefits of variable drug distribution (*continued*)

Clinical approach

Your patient, who is still suffering from nausea and vomiting despite taking carbidopa, can be helped by the antiemetic domperidone. Domperidone inhibits the emetic action of dopamine by blocking D_2 receptors in the chemoreceptor trigger zone, but it does not interfere with the central therapeutic actions of levodopa because, like carbidopa, it does not cross the blood–brain barrier to a significant degree.

nucleoproteins, and so accumulate in tissues (Table 5).

Clinical significance of drug distribution

Drug action

For a drug to have a biological effect, first it has to reach the target site of action. Lipid-insoluble drugs distribute poorly and may not reach this target site, eg lipid-insoluble aminoglycoside antibiotics are not generally used for meningitis because they transfer poorly into the CSF, even where the blood–brain barrier is damaged by inflammation.

Loading dose

Drugs that are lipid soluble, or bound to protein or tissue, distribute widely. When treatment with such drugs is started, it takes some time for lipid- or drug-binding sites to become saturated and for plasma concentrations to rise to therapeutic levels. When it is important to achieve therapeutic plasma concentrations quickly, a large first dose (loading dose) is given to saturate the lipid or binding sites of the drug rapidly. An example of this is digoxin, which is given initally as a loading dose of 500–1000 µg to achieve therapeutic plasma drug concentrations before being continued at a maintenance daily dose of 62.5–250 µg.

Drug reservoirs

Once the distribution sites of a lipid-soluble or protein- or tissue-bound drug have been saturated, the plasma concentration of the drug reaches a steady state. When administration of the drug is discontinued and the plasma concentration starts to fall through the effects of drug metabolism and excretion, the drug redistributes into the plasma from lipid or tissue reservoirs, thereby maintaining the plasma concentration. It is important to remember that the effects of such drugs may take some time to wear off, and that there is the potential for side effects or drug interactions for days or weeks after stopping the drug. Amiodarone, used for the treatment of arrhythmias, is so widely distributed and tissue bound that it takes approximately 50 days after stopping the drug for the plasma concentration to fall by half.

Drug interactions

Where two drugs that bind to the same binding site (eg plasma proteins) are given together, the binding of one or other may be reduced. The plasma concentration of the displaced drug may therefore rise, increasing the risk of drug toxicity. In practice, however, drug interactions at binding sites rarely have clinical significance.

2.4 Drug metabolism

The body 'sees' drugs as 'foreign' and attempts to expel them by metabolism and elimination. Most of these processes occur in the liver and kidneys, although other tissues and organs may play an additional role. A general principle is that drugs that are lipid soluble are difficult to excrete, because when they enter the urine or bile they are reabsorbed across cell membranes back into the body. Removal of lipid-soluble drugs from the body thus requires metabolism to make them more water soluble, followed by elimination of the metabolites in the urine or bile. Drugs that are already water soluble can be excreted without metabolism.

Drug-metabolising enzymes

Enzymes that metabolise drugs are found primarily in the smooth endoplasmic reticulum of liver cells, but also in cells of the kidney, lung and intestinal epithelium, and in the plasma. There are many different

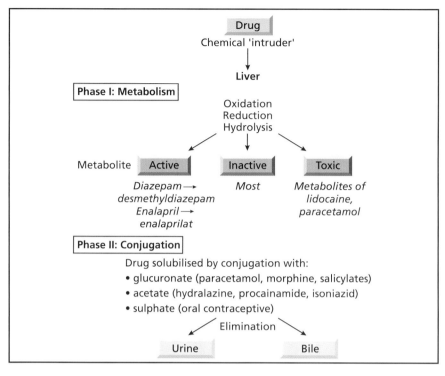

▲**Fig. 6** Drug metabolism by the liver.

types of drug-metabolising enzyme, which can be divided into those that catalyse phase I and those that catalyse phase II reactions (Fig. 6). Drugs that are metabolised by these enzymes are called substrates.

Phase I reactions

Phase I reactions make the substrate drug more polar (less lipid soluble) and may create a 'reactive' site that is susceptible to conjugation (phase II reactions). Drugs may be rendered inactive by phase I reactions,

although they may also be activated or converted to toxic metabolites (see Fig. 6). Prodrugs are inactive drugs requiring conversion to an active form by metabolism before they can exert a therapeutic effect (Table 6). Phase I reactions include the following.

- Oxidation (loss of electrons): catalysed by, for example, cytochrome P450 enzymes, oxidases, and alcohol and aldehyde dehydrogenases.

- Reduction (gain of electrons): these reactions are uncommon but include metabolism of warfarin by ketoreductase.

- Hydrolysis: catalysed insertion of an H_2O molecule into a drug, eg by esterases, proteases or peptidases. These reactions occur predominantly in the plasma.

The cytochrome P450 enzyme family

The cytochrome P450 enzyme family (CYP) is responsible for most phase I drug metabolism. There are many different CYP isoenzymes, which are grouped into families and subfamilies defined by their molecular structure, eg CYP 1A2 is a member of family 1 and subfamily A. Each isoenzyme metabolises specific substrates, although the actions of different isoenzymes may overlap. The existence of a large number of CYP isoenzymes enables the body to detoxify and excrete a wide range of exogenous compounds, as well as adapting easily to metabolise new substances. The rate of drug metabolism by CYP isoenzymes depends on genetic and environmental factors.

- Genetic factors: genetic variants of CYP isoenzymes metabolise drugs at different rates (Table 7). 'Poor metabolisers', who metabolise drugs slowly, may be particularly susceptible to the accumulation of a drug in the body and hence to side effects. 'Rapid metabolisers', who are able to clear a drug quickly, may avoid side effects but may also require larger doses of the drug to achieve the desired clinical effect.

- Environmental factors: where exposure to 'foreign' substances such as drugs, dietary components or pollutants is increased, CYP enzyme activity is induced (increased) in order to increase clearance of the substance.

TABLE 6 PRODRUGS THAT REQUIRE ACTIVATION BY THE LIVER TO EXERT AN EFFECT	
Prodrug	**Active metabolite**
Enalapril	Enalaprilat
Cyclophosphamide	Phosphoramide mustard
Azathioprine	Mercaptopurine
Zidovudine	Zidovudine triphosphate
Cortisone	Hydrocortisone
Chloral hydrate	Trichloroethanol

	Enzyme	Commonly used drugs metabolised by enzyme	Genetic variants affecting drug metabolism
Phase I reactions	CYP 2C8	Diazepam Omeprazole Barbiturates	Poor metabolisers of the CYP 2C subfamily: 20–25% of Asians
	CYP 2C18/19	Tricyclic antidepressants Diazepam Mephenytoin Omeprazole Oxicam drugs Proguanil Propranolol	Poor metabolisers: 18% of Japanese, 19% of African-Americans, 8% of Africans, 3–5% of whites
	CYP 2D6	Beta-blockers Tricyclic antidepressants SSRIs MAO-I (amiflavine) Many typical and atypical antipsychotics Many antiarrhythmics (Dihydro)codeine Ecstasy Ondansetron	Poor metabolisers: 5–10% of whites
Phase II reactions	Acetylating enzyme	Isoniazid Hydralazine Dapsone Sulfasalazine Procainamide	Rapid acetylators: 88% of Japanese, 52% of African-Americans, 48% of white Americans, approximately 35% of northern Europeans

TABLE 7 GENETIC VARIANTS OF DRUG-METABOLISING ENZYMES

MAO-I, monoamine oxidase inhibitor; SSRIs, selective serotonin reuptake inhibitors.

Conversely, CYP enzyme activity can be inhibited by drugs or dietary constituents.

> ⚠ **Dietary components that affect liver enzyme activity may interact with drugs metabolised by liver enzymes, eg constituents of grapefruit juice inhibit CYP 3A4. If patients taking drugs metabolised by CYP 3A4 (eg terfenadine) drink grapefruit juice, plasma levels of the ingested drug increase and the risk of toxic effects (prolonged QT and arrythmias with terfenadine) increases.**

Phase II reactions

Phase II reactions catalyse the coupling of a drug or polar metabolite to a substrate molecule. Conjugated drugs are inert and water soluble, and are eliminated in the urine or bile. Drugs may be conjugated with:

- glucuronate (catalysed by glucuronyl transferase);

- acetate from acetyl-CoA (catalysed by *N*-acetyltransferases);

- sulphate;

- amino acids;

- glutathione.

Genetic variants of conjugating enzymes, particularly *N*-acetyltransferases, may influence the rate of conjugating reactions (Table 7). Consider, for instance, the use of isoniazid in the treatment of tuberculosis. Isoniazid is metabolised by acetylation and excreted in the urine, its metabolites being potentially hepatotoxic. Fast acetylators, who conjugate and clear isoniazid quickly, may require increased doses for eradication of tuberculosis but are at risk of hepatotoxicity from isoniazid metabolites. Slow acetylators, who clear isoniazid more slowly, are at risk of isoniazid accumulation with peripheral neuropathy. Consider also that slow acetylators taking hydralazine or procainamide are at risk of developing antinuclear antibodies that cause a form of systemic lupus erythematosus. (See *Rheumatology and Clinical Immunology*, Sections 2.4.1 and 3.2.1.)

Example 6: Paracetamol overdose

A 17-year-old woman is admitted having taken 30 paracetamol tablets 1 hour previously. She now regrets this and denies suicidal intent. (See *Acute Medicine*, Sections 1.2.36 and 2.1.)

Clinical approach

Your main concern is that this paracetamol overdose will lead to liver damage if untreated. Prevention of liver damage depends on reducing the amount of N-acetyl-p-benzoquinone imine (NABQI), a toxic metabolite of paracetamol, available to cause hepatic necrosis. This can be done by reducing paracetamol absorption and by increasing the conjugation of NABQI.

Paracetamol pharmacokinetics

The metabolism of paracetamol (Fig. 7) illustrates that drugs are metabolised by the liver in two phases (Fig. 6). At recommended daily doses (maximum 4 g, ie eight 500-mg tablets over 24 hours), most of the paracetamol is inactivated by conjugation with glucuronate or sulphate (phase II metabolism). A small amount of paracetamol is oxidised by CYP enzymes to the reactive metabolite NABQI (phase I metabolism). This can cause cell damage, both by forming covalent bonds with cell constituents, such as key enzymes, and by generation of oxygen radicals that are cytotoxic. However, glutathione protects cells from damage by NABQI by mopping up toxic oxygen radicals and by conjugating NABQI (phase II metabolism). Both paracetamol and NABQI are made water soluble by conjugation and can be excreted in the urine.

In overdose, mechanisms that conjugate paracetamol to glucuronate or sulphate become saturated and metabolism of paracetamol to NABQI is increased (see Fig. 7). When the amount of NABQI formed is greater than the glutathione available, cell damage occurs and, as most paracetamol metabolism occurs in the liver, hepatic necrosis and hepatic failure also occur. CYP enzymes are also present in the kidney, where the generation of NABQI can result in acute tubular necrosis and renal failure.

Reducing paracetamol absorption If paracetamol absorption is reduced, less NABQI will be generated. As this patient has presented early (1 hour after taking the overdose),

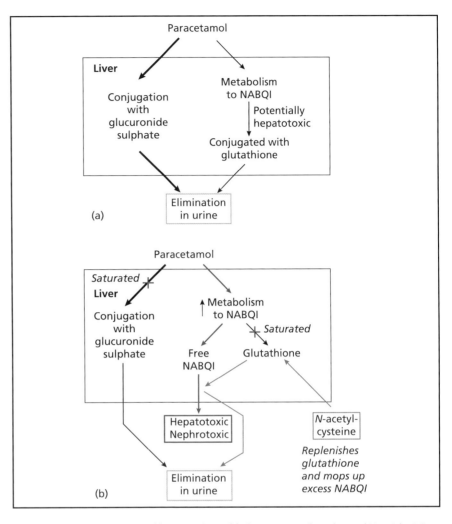

▲ Fig. 7 Paracetamol metabolism: **(a)** at normal dose; **(b)** after paracetamol overdose and N-acetylcysteine treatment.

paracetamol absorption might be reduced by oral activated charcoal. Gastric lavage may have a place in patients who have taken a large, potentially life-threatening overdose, if it is performed within 60 minutes of ingestion, but there is no convincing evidence from randomised clinical trials for the effectiveness of either gastric lavage or activated charcoal in paracetamol poisoning.

Increasing conjugation of NABQI
The aim of treatment is to increase glutathione levels so that the toxic NABQI can be conjugated. Glutathione itself cannot be given because it penetrates cells poorly. N-Acetylcysteine, which enters cells and is metabolised to glutathione, is given intravenously. (See *Acute Medicine*, Section 2.1.2.)

Time course of drug metabolism by enzymes

First-order metabolism

The rate of drug metabolism by most drug-metabolising enzymes increases in direct proportion to the concentration of drug available, and therefore a constant fraction of the drug available will be processed (Fig. 8). Increasing or decreasing the dose of a drug metabolised by first-order processes will result in a predictable change in plasma concentration.

Zero-order metabolism

Some drug-metabolising enzymes become saturated as the concentration of the drug increases.

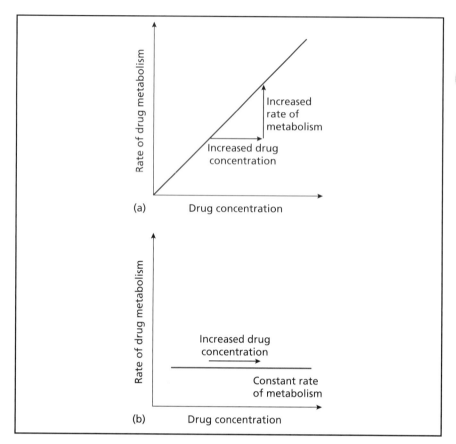

▲ **Fig. 8** (a) First-order and (b) zero-order kinetics.

Once this saturation point has been reached, the enzyme can metabolise a constant amount of the drug, but a further increase in the available drug does not result in increased processing of the drug (Fig. 8). When a drug is metabolised by a zero-order process, a dose increase will result in a large and disproportionate increase in plasma concentration, which has the potential to produce toxicity. Removal of excessive amounts of a drug from the body, eg after an overdose, is also slow where metabolism is by zero-order processes. The main examples of drugs metabolised by zero-order processes are ethanol and phenytoin.

Time course of other pharmacokinetic processes

Other pharmacokinetic processes, including absorption, distribution and elimination, may exhibit either zero- or first-order kinetics. For example, drug absorption across cell membranes by transport proteins could be a first-order process if absorption increases with increased drug concentration, or it could be a zero-order process if drug transfer by the transport protein becomes saturated.

Cytochrome P450 enzymes and drug interactions

Drug interactions with the CYP system are shown in Table 8, which also shows other substrates for liver enzymes that have a narrow therapeutic range. Note that in some cases the presence of the disease process narrows the therapeutic window.

Enzyme inhibition

Example 7: An interaction leading to theophylline toxicity

A 65-year-old man who is taking theophylline for chronic obstructive pulmonary disease is admitted with convulsions. He has recently started taking ciprofloxacin for a chest infection.

Clinical approach

You are concerned that the convulsions in this patient are caused by theophylline toxicity, precipitated by concurrent therapy with ciprofloxacin.

Theophylline metabolism

Theophylline is cleared from the body by CYP 1A2 metabolism followed by conjugation and elimination. Ciprofloxacin inhibits the actions of CYP 1A2, so if a patient who is already receiving theophylline starts taking ciprofloxacin, theophylline metabolism will be reduced and theophylline plasma concentrations will rise, an interaction that is clinically significant because theophylline has a narrow therapeutic range (Fig. 9). This narrow therapeutic range means that the plasma concentration of theophylline that has a therapeutic effect is only slightly lower than the theophylline concentration that will cause toxic effects such as nausea, irritability, dysrhythmias and convulsions. Thus, a relatively small decrease in theophylline metabolism will cause an increase in theophylline concentration sufficient to cause toxicity. In addition to its effect on theophylline metabolism, ciprofloxacin may also independently lower seizure thresholds, thereby further increasing the likelihood of seizures in this patient.

A different clinical approach to avoid the problem

In this patient, theophylline toxicity could have been prevented if he had been given a different antibiotic instead of ciprofloxacin, eg amoxicillin, which does not inhibit liver enzymes. If treatment with ciprofloxacin or

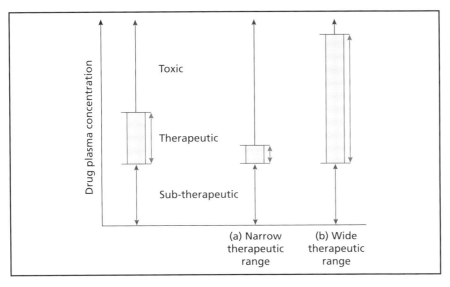

▲ **Fig. 9** Therapeutic range describes the plasma concentrations at which a drug exerts a safe therapeutic effect. (**a**) Where the range is narrow, therapeutic plasma concentrations are close to toxic plasma concentrations, and a small change in dose or drug metabolism may precipitate drug toxicity. (**b**) Where the range is wide, therapeutic plasma concentrations are much lower than toxic concentrations, and toxicity is unlikely.

FURTHER READING

For a more comprehensive table of drugs that are substrates for, or inhibitors/inducers of, CYP enzymes, see the Indiana University School of Medicine website at http://medicine.iupui.edu/flockhart/table.htm

– – – – – – – – – – – – – – – – – –

For further information on poisoning, try the Guy's and St Thomas' Poisons Unit website at http://www.medtox.org/

– – – – – – – – – – – – – – – – – –

The National Poisons Information Service website is available at http://www.spib.axl.co.uk/ (note that you or your hospital will need to register to use TOXBASE)

TABLE 8 DRUG INTERACTIONS AND THE CYP SYSTEM

CYP substrates with narrow therapeutic range	Drugs that inhibit CYP enzymes	Drugs that induce CYP enzymes
Warfarin	Cimetidine	Phenytoin
Theophylline	Ciprofloxacin	Phenobarbital
Ciclosporin	Erythromycin	Carbamazepine
Ethinylestradiol	Sodium valproate	Rifampicin
Phenytoin	Isoniazid	Griseofulvin
	Omeprazole	Alcohol
	Fluoxetine	Tobacco smoke
	Fluconazole	Primidone
		Sulfinpyrazone

2.5 Drug elimination

Example 8: Slowing drug elimination can make treatment simpler

A 22-year-old man of no fixed abode attends a walk-in genitourinary clinic complaining of dysuria and urethral discharge. He requires treatment for gonorrhoea.

Clinical approach

Your main concern is to ensure treatment for his gonorrhoea to:

• prevent worsening illness;
• prevent its spread to any of his sexual contacts.

You wish to give him a course of amoxicillin, but given his social circumstances you are concerned that he may have problems following a treatment regimen or attending for follow-up.

erythromycin (which also inhibits liver enzymes) was unavoidable, then a reduction in theophylline dosage should have been considered during antibiotic treatment.

⚠ Theophylline toxicity may be precipitated by the co-administration of ciprofloxacin or erythromycin, both of which inhibit liver enzyme activity and reduce theophylline metabolism.

Enzyme induction

Drugs that induce liver enzymes increase the metabolism of drugs that are substrates for the same enzymes (Table 8), causing a fall in plasma concentration of the substrate drug that may reduce its therapeutic effect. A classic example of this type of drug interaction is seen where rifampicin and the combined oral contraceptive pill are co-administered: rifampicin induces CYP enzymes that metabolise oestrogen, resulting in a fall in plasma oestrogen levels and loss of contraceptive effect.

TABLE 9 ROUTES OF DRUG ELIMINATION

Excretion route	Comment
Urine	Most drugs
Faeces	Biliary excretion (see Fig. 6) Unabsorbed drug passes out in faeces
Lung	Exhaled drugs, eg volatile anaesthetics, ethanol, paraldehyde
Breast milk	A small amount of most drugs appears in breast milk, but contributes little to elimination

Pharmacokinetics of drug elimination

Drugs are eliminated from the body by a number of routes (Table 9). To be eliminated by the kidney the drug must pass into the urine (Fig. 10), which takes place by:

- glomerular filtration (drugs of molecular weight <20,000);

- active transport by cation or anion transporters, which pump the drug into the urine across the renal tubular epithelium.

In addition, drugs must be lipid insoluble to remain in the urine and not be reabsorbed in the renal tubule.

Clearance

Renal clearance is defined as the volume of plasma that contains the amount of drug cleared from the body in a unit of time. This depends on the glomerular filtration rate (GFR) and the mechanisms of transport of the drug into and out of the renal tubule. Examples are shown below.

Gallamine This is a non-depolarising neuromuscular blocking agent (muscle relaxant), which is now rarely used. It is still notable because it enters the urine by glomerular filtration but is not reabsorbed or secreted in the renal tubules; hence the renal clearance of gallamine will be the same as the GFR. If the GFR is 120 mL/min, then 120 mL of plasma will be completely cleared of gallamine every minute.

Penicillin Approximately 20% of the penicillin delivered to the glomeruli is filtered into the urine. The other 80% remains in the plasma and passes in the efferent arterioles to the renal tubules. Anion transporters in the renal tubules actively secrete this penicillin into the urine. The blood passing through the kidney is thus almost completely cleared of penicillin and its renal clearance is much greater than the GFR. Approximately 480 mL of plasma are cleared of penicillin every minute.

Diazepam Diazepam is lipid soluble, so most of the diazepam excreted into the urine is reabsorbed back into the blood. Excretion of diazepam is very slow and clearance is much less than the GFR.

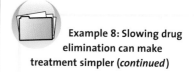

Example 8: Slowing drug elimination can make treatment simpler (*continued*)

Clinical approach

Amoxicillin is commonly effective against gonorrhoea and could be useful in this patient. However, its renal clearance is extremely rapid because it is actively secreted into the renal tubule by anion transporters and it has a half-life of less than 2 hours. Amoxicillin alone is therefore not ideal as a single-dose treatment to eradicate gonococci. The renal clearance of amoxicillin can be reduced by giving it with probenecid, which competes for the anion transporter and thus reduces

---

1 Glomerular filtration

Drugs — molecular weight < 20 000 (ie **not** heparin, dextran, protein hormones, growth factors)

Less drug filtered if highly bound to plasma protein, eg warfarin

2 Active secretion

Anion transporters
Acidic drugs, eg
Penicillin
Acetazolamide
Aminosalicylic acid
Salicylic acid
Cephalosporins
Furosemide (frusemide)
Thiazides
Methotrexate
Contrast media

Anion transporters inhibited by probenecid

Cation transporters
Basic drugs, eg
Amiloride
Triamterene
Dopamine
Morphine
Pethidine
Quinine

3 Passive movement

Reabsorption of lipid-soluble drugs

Diffusion into tubule

Elimination

▲ **Fig. 10** Mechanisms of renal drug elimination.

the secretion of amoxicillin into the renal tubule and increases its duration of action. A single dose of amoxicillin 3 g with probenecid 1 g has been shown to cure over 98% of men with uncomplicated gonococcal urethritis. Probenecid also delays excretion and prolongs the action of other drugs secreted by the anion transporter (eg cephalosporins).

2.6 Plasma half-life and steady-state plasma concentrations

Example 9: A side effect of digoxin

A 72-year-old man taking digoxin 250 μg daily for atrial fibrillation complains of nausea, which is attributed to mild digoxin excess. The dose of digoxin is reduced to 125 μg daily, but the next day his nausea persists.

Clinical approach

Adjustment of his digoxin dose requires knowledge of pharmacokinetic principles.

Pharmacokinetics

Plasma concentration

As soon as a drug is absorbed into the plasma, removal from the plasma commences, the plasma concentration of the drug being the sum of the processes of absorption, distribution, metabolism and elimination. The plasma concentration of a drug is important because this is the major determinant of the concentration of a drug at the target site. The aim of therapy is to achieve a plasma concentration above the

minimum effective concentration but below the minimum toxic concentration (see Fig. 9).

Half-life

The plasma half-life ($t_{1/2}$) of a drug is defined as the time taken for the plasma concentration of a drug to fall by half. Drugs removed from the plasma rapidly have a short half-life, eg amoxicillin is rapidly cleared by the renal tubules and has a half-life of about 2 hours. Drugs removed from the plasma slowly have a long half-life, eg diazepam is slowly eliminated by the kidney and has a $t_{1/2}$ of about 40 hours.

Steady-state plasma concentrations

After a single dose of a drug is given and absorbed, it is removed from the plasma almost completely over a time equivalent to four to five half-lives of that drug (Fig. 11). Where repeat doses of the drug are given, the average plasma concentration of the drug increases until drug absorption and removal are in equilibrium and a steady-state plasma concentration is reached. Where a consistent dosing regimen is used, steady-state plasma

concentrations will be achieved after five half-lives of the drug (Fig. 12).

Drug dose and dose interval

For a given dosing regimen it will always take five half-lives of the drug to reach a steady-state plasma concentration of that drug. However, the level of the steady-state plasma concentration achieved in an individual will be determined not only by the drug dosing regimen but also by the clearance rate of the drug (Table 10). Thus higher plasma concentrations will result from excessive dosage or reduced clearance, whereas lower plasma concentrations can be caused by inadequate dosage or increased clearance (Table 10). Once the steady-state plasma concentration has been reached, the plasma concentration will only be maintained continuously at this concentration if the drug is given by intravenous infusion at a constant rate (eg heparin or insulin). If the drug is given intermittently (eg oral digoxin once daily or intravenous gentamicin three times daily), the plasma concentration will swing around the steady-state concentration, with the magnitude of the swings for

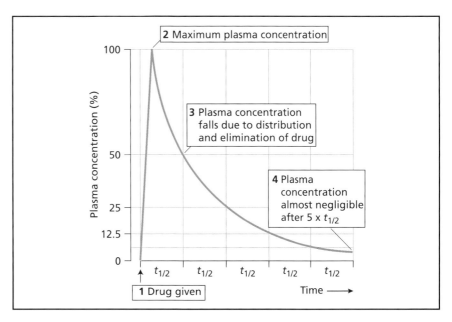

▲ **Fig. 11** Plasma half-life ($t_{1/2}$) of a drug: plasma concentration after a single dose.

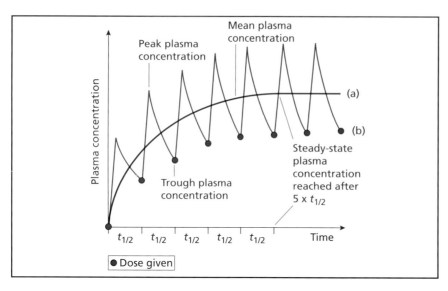

▲ **Fig. 12** Steady-state plasma concentration: plasma concentration after repeated dosing. For a constant dosing regimen, the plasma drug concentration reaches a steady state after a time equivalent to five half-lives of the drug. If the drug is given by continuous intravenous infusion (**a**), there is no fluctuation in plasma concentration around this level. However, where a drug is given intermittently (**b**) the plasma concentration swings from peak concentration shortly after the dose to trough concentration just before the next dose. The magnitude of the swings is determined by the dose interval.

TABLE 10 FACTORS AFFECTING PLASMA CONCENTRATION OF DRUG ACHIEVED FOR A GIVEN DOSING REGIMEN	
Reduced plasma concentration	**Increased plasma concentration**
Poor compliance/adherence	Drugs taken in overdose
Poor drug absorption	Augmented drug absorption
High first-pass metabolism	Low or impaired first-pass metabolism
Increased activity of drug-metabolising enzymes Induction by other drug Genetic hypermetabolism	Reduced activity of drug-metabolising enzymes Inhibition by other drugs Genetic hypometabolism
	Liver failure
	Renal failure
	Extremes of age (neonate or very old)

a given dose of drug being determined by the dosing interval (Fig. 12).

Example 9: A side effect of digoxin (*continued*)

Clinical approach

Digoxin has a $t_{1/2}$ of around 36 hours, so it will take approximately 7.5 days ($5 \times t_{1/2}$) for the plasma concentration of digoxin in your patient to fall to a new steady-state level after this dose reduction. You would therefore expect his symptoms to resolve over several days.

2.7 Drug monitoring

Example 9: A side effect of digoxin (*continued*)

At a follow-up appointment 3 weeks later, the patient continues to have nausea and is also having frequent nose-bleeds. On questioning, he is unclear which tablets he is taking, but has packets of tablets containing digoxin 250 µg and warfarin 5 mg.

Clinical approach

Your main concerns are:

- his nausea may be caused by digoxin toxicity;
- his nose-bleeds may indicate excessive anticoagulation by warfarin.

You need to check these suspicions by drug monitoring.

Monitoring drug therapy

Every patient who takes any medication should be 'monitored' for:

- drug effectiveness;
- drug toxicity.

Monitoring can be carried out by the following:

- subjective reporting by the patient, eg relief of symptoms or complaints of side effects;
- measurement of the effects of a drug (pharmacodynamic monitoring), eg blood pressure in patients taking antihypertensives, plasma cholesterol concentration in a patient taking a statin or INR measurement in a patient taking warfarin;
- measurement of plasma concentration of drug (pharmacokinetic monitoring).

Measurement of drug plasma concentration

The monitoring of drug concentration in plasma is only useful under the following circumstances.

- The drug concentration can be measured accurately and there are no significant pharmacologically active metabolites that are not measured.
- The plasma concentration reflects drug action, ie a therapeutic range

TABLE 11 DRUGS COMMONLY MONITORED BY PLASMA CONCENTRATION MEASUREMENT

Drug	$t_{1/2}$ (hours)	Purpose of monitoring	Timing of measurement	Time to steady state
Digoxin	36	Therapeutic? Toxic?	At least 6 hours after dose or immediately before dose	7 days (longer in renal failure)
Lithium	22 ($\pm$8)	Therapeutic? Toxic?	12 hours after dose	3–7 days
Phenytoin	6–24	Therapeutic? Toxic?	Immediately prior to next dose	7 days or longer (variable)
Aminoglycosides, eg gentamicin (given iv tds)	2–3	Therapeutic? Toxic?	Trough: immediately before next dose Peak: 30 minutes post dose	12–40 hours (longer in renal failure)

can be defined below which levels are likely to be subtherapeutic and above which drug levels are likely to have toxic effects (see Fig. 9).

- The therapeutic or toxic effects of the drug cannot be measured more simply and reliably by clinical measurements (as above).

Drug concentrations vary in the plasma between doses, being lowest just before a dose and highest shortly after a dose (see Fig. 12). Therefore, the timing of sampling for measurement of plasma concentration must be considered carefully in the interpretation of plasma drug levels. Examples of drugs that are commonly monitored by measuring plasma concentrations are shown in Table 11.

Example 9: A side effect of digoxin (*continued*)

Digoxin

Measurement of plasma digoxin concentration will be useful in this patient in order to determine whether his nausea is caused by digoxin toxicity. Where the dosing regimen is known, sampling for measurement of digoxin concentration should be done between 6 and 18 hours after the last dose. The measured concentration can then be compared against values that define therapeutic and toxic levels. In this patient a 'random' digoxin level should be measured because the time of the last dose is not known. Note also that it is very important to take blood for a potassium concentration at the same time as the digoxin

concentration is measured, because it is possible to have digoxin toxicity with a digoxin concentration within the notional therapeutic range when there is coexistent hypokalaemia.

Warfarin

Nose-bleeds in a patient on warfarin may be caused by excessive anticoagulation. Direct measurement of the effect of warfarin using the INR is more useful than trying to measure warfarin plasma levels.

FURTHER READING

Aronson JK, Hardman M and Reynolds DJM. *ABC of Monitoring Drug Therapy*. London: BMJ Publishing Group, 1993.

This aspect of clinical pharmacology is concerned with how drugs exert their effects on the body. An understanding of the mechanism of drug action provides insights into expected benefits and adverse effects, and whether a drug is likely to enhance or limit the action of a second agent. This understanding can also enable prediction of the likely effects of a disease process on the response to a drug, and how the action of a drug might be altered as a result of changes in normal physiology, eg during pregnancy or at the extremes of age.

In the past, the therapeutic properties of compounds were identified empirically. Examples include aspirin, digoxin and glyceryl trinitrate. Today, a more systematic approach to drug design is taken. Studies of physiology and pathophysiology are used to identify new therapeutic targets for which novel compounds are then synthesised (Table 12).

3.1 How drugs exert their effects

Most drugs act by binding to proteins in the body, thereby activating, inhibiting or in some way modifying their normal function (Fig. 13 and Table 13). The most important classes of drug target are:

- membrane or cytoplasmic receptors for endogenous signalling molecules such as hormones and neurotransmitters;
- enzymes;
- ion channels;
- transporters of small molecules, such as amino acids.

Not all drugs target proteins. Examples of those that do not include the following.

- General anaesthetics: act by altering the properties of the lipid membrane of neurons.

- Oxygen: an important and widely prescribed drug. It receives electrons transported along the mitochondrial respiratory chain as part of cellular respiration.
- Lactulose (which is not absorbed) and mannitol (which is absorbed): act by altering the osmotic balance in the bowel lumen and vascular compartment, respectively.
- Antacids: neutralise gastric contents.
- Cholestyramine (a bile acid-binding resin): lowers cholesterol by inhibiting its enterohepatic recirculation.

Knowing the nature of the drug target and its role in normal physiology enables some predictions to be made about the amount of drug required to exert an effect and how quickly the effect will occur. Drugs that target membrane surface receptors for hormones or neurotransmitters have a rapid action, particularly if the drug is delivered by the intravenous route and targets a surface receptor that is coupled to a rapidly acting signal transduction cascade or an ion channel. For other drugs, although the interaction of the drug with its target may be rapid, the onset of the therapeutic effect can be delayed because the kinetics of the system that is affected are slow.

The development of biologicals (monoclonal antibodies targeting cell-surface receptors or selected mediators) has resulted in a rapid increase in available therapeutic targets. Agents now exist that target a number of endogenous receptors, such as:

TABLE 12 NEWLY INTRODUCED DRUGS TARGETING NOVEL TARGETS		
Drug	**Target**	**Use**
Sildenafil	Phosphodiesterase type V	Erectile impotence
Abciximab	Platelet glycoprotein IIb/IIIa receptor	Inhibition of thrombosis following coronary stent insertion
Simvastatin	HMG-CoA reductase	Hypercholesterolaemia
Montelukast	Cysteinyl leukotriene receptor	Asthma
Losartan	Angiotensin II receptor	Hypertension and heart failure
Infliximab	Tumour necrosis factor	Systemic inflammatory disorders, eg rheumatoid arthritis

HMG-CoA, hydroxymethylglutaryl coenzyme A.

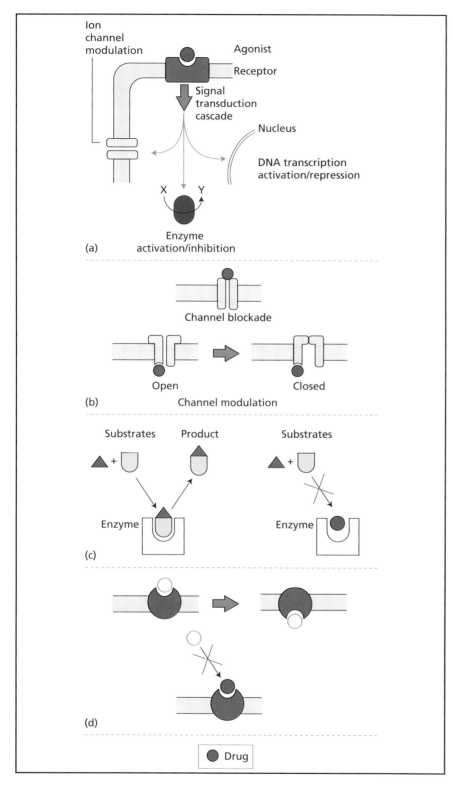

▲ **Fig. 13** Molecular targets for drugs. The major targets for drugs are cellular proteins, including (**a**) membrane receptors, (**b**) ion channels, (**c**) enzymes and (**d**) transporters.

- ranibizumab, a monoclonal antibody that inhibits vascular endothelial growth factor, used in the treatment of wet age-related macular degeneration;

- trastuzumab (Herceptin), a monoclonal antibody that inhibits the human epidermal growth factor receptor (HER2), used in the treatment of breast cancer;

- rituximab, an anti-CD20 monoclonal antibody used in the treatement of non-Hodgkin's lymphoma.

It is important that such biological compounds are evaluated with the same rigour as conventional small molecules to ensure their safety.

Example 10: Rapid treatment of a rapid pulse

A fit 30-year-old woman with a history of episodic self-terminating palpitations attends the Emergency Department with a further, more prolonged episode. She is haemodynamically stable and her ECG reveals a regular, narrow and complex tachycardia with a rate of 180 bpm. Carotid sinus massage is ineffective.

Clinical approach

The probable diagnosis here is an atrioventricular (AV) re-entrant or AV nodal re-entrant tachycardia, the substrate being a re-entrant circuit involving the AV node. These dysrhythmias can therefore be terminated by producing transient AV nodal blockade of even a few seconds' duration. Vagotonic manoeuvres (eg carotid sinus massage) are usually tried first but, if ineffective, the drug of choice is adenosine. Adenosine binds G-protein-coupled adenosine receptors on the surface of conducting cells in the AV node, which results in the rapid opening of membrane K^+ channels, hyperpolarisation and conduction block. When given by fast intravenous injection the onset of effect is rapid, occurring within seconds. Furthermore, the effects of adenosine are extremely short-lived because the drug is rapidly removed from the circulation by carrier-mediated uptake and metabolism in endothelial cells. Rapid uptake and inactivation do not compromise the effect of the drug and are advantageous because they minimise side effects. However, this requires that the drug be administered by fast intravenous bolus.

TABLE 13 TARGETS AND DRUGS THAT BIND THEM

		Drug	
	Target	Agonist	Antagonist
Receptor	ACh nicotinic (ganglionic)	–	Trimetaphan
	ACh nicotinic (NMJ)	Suxamethonium	D-Tubocurarine
	ACh muscarinic	Pilocarpine	Atropine, ipratropium, hyoscine, orphenadrine
	α_1-Adrenoceptor	Norepinephrine (noradrenaline) Epinephrine (adrenaline)	Phentolamine, doxazosin, prazosin
	α_2-Adrenoceptor	Clonidine, brimonidine	Phentolamine
	β_1-Adrenoceptor	Epinephrine (adrenaline), isoprenaline, dobutamine	Propranolol, atenolol, bisoprolol
	β_2-Adrenoceptor	Salbutamol, terbutaline	Propranolol, timolol
	$5HT_1$	Sumatriptan	Methysergide
	$5HT_3$	–	
	Dopamine D_2	Bromocriptine, lisuride, pergolide	Domperidone, metoclopramide, chlorpromazine
	Histamine H_1	–	Chlorpheniramine
	Histamine H_2	–	Cimetidine, ranitidine
	Mineralocorticoid	Fludrocortisone	Spironolactone
	Vasopressin	Glypressin	–
	Somatostatin	Octreotide	–
	Angiotensin II	–	Losartan
	Platelet glycoprotein IIb/IIIa	–	Abciximab
	Cysteinyl leukotriene	–	Montelukast, zafirlukast
Enzyme	*Target*	*Inhibitor*	
	Cholinesterase	Neostigmine, pyridostigmine, edrophonium	
	COX	Aspirin, NSAIDs	
	COX-2	Rofecoxib, celecoxib	
	Xanthine oxidase	Allopurinol	
	ACE	Captopril, enalapril, lisinopril	
	HMG-CoA reductase	Simvastatin, pravastatin	
	MAO-A	Pargyline, isocarboxazid, moclobemide	
	MAO-B	Selegiline	
Carriers	Uptake 1	Tricyclics, cocaine	
	Weak acids	Probenecid	
	$Na^+/K^+/Cl^-$ cotransporter	Furosemide, bumetanide	
	Na^+/K^+-ATPase	Digoxin	
	H^+-ATPase	Omeprazole, esomeprazole	
Nuclear transcription factors	Oestrogen receptor	Raloxifene[1]	
	PPAR α	Clofibrate, gemfibrozil	
	PPAR γ	Rosiglitazone, pioglitazone	

1. Raloxifene is an example of a selective oestrogen receptor modulator and can act either as an oestrogen receptor agonist or antagonist, depending on the tissue it is acting upon. Other drugs in this class include tamoxifen and clomiphene.

ACE, angiotensin-converting enzyme; ACh, acetylcholine; COX, cyclooxygenase; HMG-CoA, hydroxymethylglutaryl coenzyme A; 5HT, 5-hydroxytryptamine; MAO, monoamine oxidase; NMJ, neuromuscular junction; PPAR, peroxisome proliferator-activated receptor.

Example 11: Thyrotoxicosis: how fast will it get better?

A 61-year-old woman with a 6-month history of weight loss, palpitations, tremor and heat intolerance is diagnosed as having primary thyrotoxicosis caused by Graves' disease. She is concerned about whether her treatment will result in the prompt resolution of symptoms.

Clinical approach

The aims of treatment are to relieve symptoms and to render the patient euthyroid. Thionamides (eg carbimazole and propylthiouracil) inhibit the formation of thyroid hormones by interfering with the incorporation of iodine into the tyrosyl residues of thyroglobulin. This is achieved by inhibition of the peroxidase enzyme, which catalyses this reaction. Synthesis of a new hormone is inhibited, but the full therapeutic effect may not be seen until stores of the preformed hormone have been depleted, which can take 6–8 weeks. During this time, the symptoms of tremor and palpitations can be treated by a non-selective beta-blocker such as propranolol. In the long term the definitive treatment of this woman's condition might be with radioiodine.

FURTHER READING

Grahame-Smith DG and Aronson JK. *Oxford Textbook of Clinical Pharmacology and Drug Therapy*, 3rd edn. Oxford: Oxford University Press, 2002.

3.2 Selectivity is the key to the therapeutic utility of an agent

For a drug to be clinically useful, it should be capable of modifying a particular function in a particular cell or tissue without altering related or unrelated functions elsewhere in the body. In the best case, the action of a drug would be restricted solely to the target organ or tissue. Rather inconveniently, many of the common targets for drugs, such as membrane receptors or ion channels, are widely distributed, often in diverse organs or tissues (Fig. 14). For this reason, the therapeutic goal of absolute selectivity is, in practice, difficult to attain.

Selectivity of action from localised delivery of a drug

On occasion, the aim of selectivity can be achieved by delivery of the drug locally to its desired site of action. This is feasible for drugs that act on the skin, eye, airways, and upper and lower gastrointestinal tract. However, if significant absorption occurs from the site of local delivery, systemic side effects may still result.

Example 12: A systemic effect of local treatment

A 74-year-old woman who smokes is found by her optician to have an intraocular pressure of 28 mmHg in both eyes, an arcuate visual field defect and disc cupping compatible with a diagnosis of primary open-angle glaucoma. After ophthalmological referral, she is prescribed timolol eye drops. At the 6-week follow-up the intraocular pressure in both eyes has fallen to 19 mmHg, but she complains of tiredness, low mood and difficulty

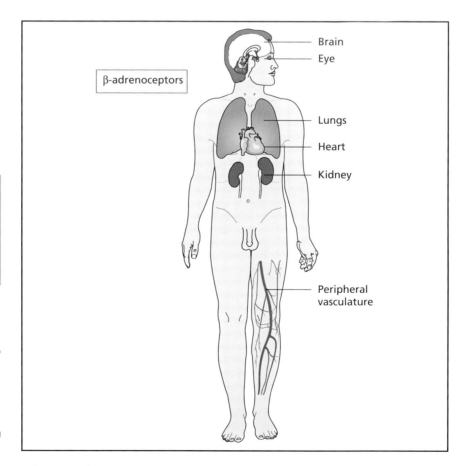

▲ **Fig. 14** Some drug targets are distributed widely: β-adrenoceptors can be found in the brain, eye, lungs, heart, kidney and blood vessels.

climbing stairs. Respiratory examination reveals bilateral polyphonic wheezes and her peak expiratory flow rate is 150 L/min.

Clinical approach

This patient is likely to be manifesting side effects from timolol, a non-selective beta-blocker that may be absorbed from the ocular surface and which blocks β receptors in the lungs and brain (Figs 14 and 15). Note that:

- β_2-adrenoceptor blockade in the small airways may unmask an undiagnosed asthmatic component to chronic obstructive airway disease in a smoker, and many studies have documented worsening of pulmonary function in elderly patients treated with timolol eye drops, although the incidence of frank respiratory symptoms is low;
- timolol is also lipid soluble and can therefore cross the blood–brain barrier, where symptoms arising from β blockade include tiredness, depression, poor sleep and nightmares.

An alternative clinical approach

Fortunately, alternative treatments are available for the treatment of primary open-angle glaucoma and include brimonidine (an α_2-adrenoceptor agonist), dorzolamide (a carbonic anhydrase inhibitor), latanoprost (a prostaglandin analogue) and pilocarpine (a muscarinic cholinoceptor agonist).

Corticosteroids are commonly administered locally to limit systemic side effects. Sites of delivery include the ocular surface (for allergic and inflammatory eye disease), the airways (for asthma), the skin (for eczema), and the rectum and colon (for ulcerative colitis and Crohn's disease). However, suppression of adrenocortical function and effects on bone mineral metabolism may still be observed, particularly if high dosages are used.

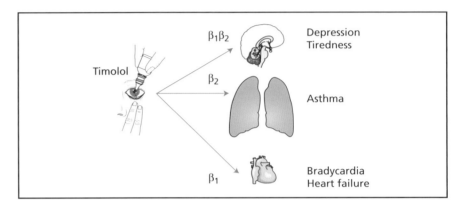

▲ **Fig. 15** Systemic absorption from the site of local delivery can result in side effects.

Pharmacological selectivity

Selectivity of action is most commonly achieved by using drugs with a particular affinity for receptor, channel or enzyme subtypes, the expression of which is restricted to the cells or tissue of interest. In the best case, the concentration of drug required to modify the target receptor subtype may be many orders of magnitude lower than that at which related receptor subtypes are bound. However, complete selectivity is rarely achieved and many of the adverse effects of drugs result from their interaction with related receptors, enzymes or ion channels located at distant sites.

Example 13: Unwanted dizziness

A 78-year-old man with hesitancy, poor urinary stream and nocturia is diagnosed as having bladder outflow tract obstruction from benign prostatic hyperplasia. He is prescribed doxazosin with good relief of his urinary symptoms, but he complains of dizziness on standing, particularly when getting out of bed in the morning.

Clinical approach

In benign prostatic hyperplasia, urinary outflow obstruction is partly structural and partly functional, the latter

resulting from tonic α_1-adrenoceptor-mediated contraction of smooth muscle in the bladder neck, prostatic capsule and prostatic urethra. α_1-Adrenoceptor antagonists (such as prazosin, doxazosin and torazosin) improve symptoms in this disorder by causing relaxation of smooth muscle at these sites. However, the major side effect of this group of drugs is postural hypotension caused by blockade of α_1-adrenoceptors in the smooth muscle of small arteries, which results in reduction in peripheral resistance and hence a fall in blood pressure (Fig. 16). Guidance about rising slowly from a lying position or when getting out of a chair may be all that is required, but finasteride (a 5α-reductase inhibitor that prevents the conversion of testosterone to dihydrotestosterone and reduces prostatic volume) could be used as an alternative to doxazosin. Its therapeutic effects are seen after several months of therapy.

Traditionally, receptor subtypes were classified in functional terms on the basis of similarities and differences in response to agonists and antagonists (see below). More recently, with the advent of recombinant DNA technology, receptors have come to be redefined in structural terms on the basis of their DNA and amino acid sequences. Related receptors (receptor families) are sometimes the products of distinct but structurally similar

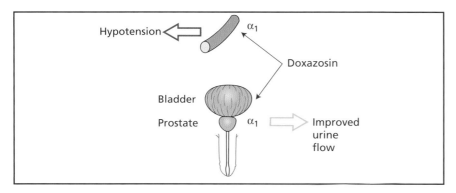

▲ **Fig. 16** Binding of a drug to its target results in the therapeutic response, but binding to related proteins elsewhere can lead to side effects.

genes or, occasionally, are encoded by the same gene with structural differences introduced at the level of mRNA processing.

Example 14: A patient who had not read the literature

A 58-year-old man with stable New York Heart Association (NYHA) grade III heart failure from dilated cardiomyopathy, treated with furosemide and ramipril, is started on a low dose of bisoprolol in the light of studies that have demonstrated mortality reductions with low-dose β blockade in patients with mild to moderate heart failure. One week after the start of treatment, he complains of breathlessness, there are basal crackles in his lungs and a CXR shows upper lobe blood diversion and Kerley B lines.

Clinical approach

Patients with heart failure exhibit compensatory activation of the sympathetic nervous system, which helps maintain cardiac output in the face of impaired myocardial performance. In the long term, this heightened sympathetic drive may have deleterious effects on cardiac myocytes and may promote dysrhythmias. The mechanism by which beta-blockers reduce mortality in patients with heart failure is unknown, but may be related to an antiarrhythmic effect that is mediated by blockade of β_1-adrenoceptors on myocardial cells and in conducting tissue. Beta-blockers should be started

at low dose in patients with heart failure, because their negative inotropic effects may result in a rapid reduction in cardiac output, which can worsen heart failure and even cause pulmonary oedema. Any dosage increase should be made slowly and conducted under specialist supervision. If there is deterioration in the symptoms or any signs of heart failure, the dose of beta-blocker should be reduced and the dose of diuretic and angiotensin-converting enzyme inhibitor increased (if possible). A subsequent increase in the dose of beta-blocker (to the maintenance dosage used in recent trials) may then be possible.

When using beta-blockers in patients with heart failure, be aware of the narrow therapeutic window.

- Ensure that the condition is stable and that the patient has heart failure in NYHA grade II or III.
- Use bisoprolol two or carvedilol (currently the only beta-blocker licensed for this indication in the UK) because these are the agents that have been evaluated in clinical trials.
- Start at a low dose and titrate the dose upwards with care ('Start Low, Go Slow'): the daily dosing schedule for carvedilol is 3.125 mg initially, increasing to 6.25 mg after 1 week, 12.5 mg after 3 weeks, 25 mg after 5 weeks and 50 mg after 7 weeks.
- Ensure frequent follow-up and active monitoring for clinical deterioration.

3.3 Basic aspects of the interaction of a drug with its target

Agonists and the dose–response curve

Many of the principles of drug action were developed around the interaction of drug molecules with membrane receptors. The term 'agonist' is given to a drug that binds to a receptor to produce the same biological response as the receptor's natural ligand. In most cases, the binding of a drug to its receptor is a reversible process and the degree of receptor activation, which is related to the number of receptors bound by a drug at any one time, is proportional to the concentration of drug in the vicinity of the receptor. A graph that depicts the relationship between the logarithm of the concentration of an agonist drug and the proportion of the maximal biological effect produced is called a log concentration–response curve and is sigmoid in shape. As the concentration of drug is related to the dose administered, the terms 'concentration–response curve' and 'dose–response curve' are sometimes used interchangeably (Fig. 17).

For some drugs, the dose administered provides a local concentration close to that required for the maximal therapeutic response, in which case increasing the dose of drug confers no additional therapeutic benefit. It may increase the likelihood of side effects, the incidence of which may be more closely dependent on dose (Fig. 18).

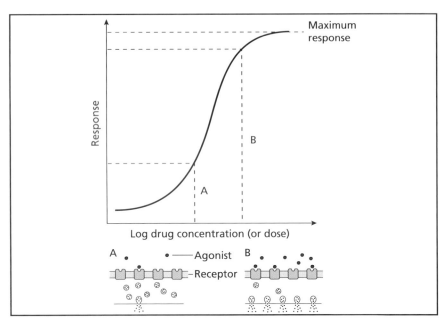

▲**Fig. 17** Relationship between drug dose and response. Increasing the concentration of drug (A–B) results in an enhanced response.

Potency, efficacy and partial agonists

A potent agonist drug is one that is capable of producing the maximal response from a tissue at a low concentration. Ultimately, the maximum possible biological response that can be elicited from a tissue is determined not by the potency of the drug but by the capacity of the tissue to respond. For instance, once the receptors that activate the secretion of a neurotransmitter are maximally bound by their activating ligand, the maximum amount of neurotransmitter released will be determined by the level of the intracellular stores. For this reason, a drug of low potency is capable of producing the same maximum

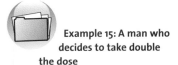

Example 15: A man who decides to take double the dose

A 65-year-old man with uncomplicated essential hypertension is prescribed bendroflumethiazide 2.5 mg daily by his doctor and elects to purchase an automated home BP-recording device. After several BP recordings of around 165/105 mmHg, he decides to double the dose of bendroflumethiazide. On review in the surgery 4 weeks later, his BP is 168/108 mmHg and his serum K+ 2.2 mmol/L.

Clinical approach

In this patient the increase in dose of bendroflumethiazide from 2.5 to 5 mg fails to produce a reduction in BP but does cause hypokalaemia. Other metabolic side effects of bendroflumethiazide (eg hyperglycaemia, hyperuricaemia and elevations in serum lipids) are also more common with higher doses. For patients whose BP remains poorly controlled with low-dose bendroflumethiazide, introduction of a second antihypertensive agent (eg a beta-blocker or angiotensin-converting enzyme inhibitor), the actions of which are synergistic with those of the thiazide diuretic, will usually result in adequate BP control with fewer side effects.

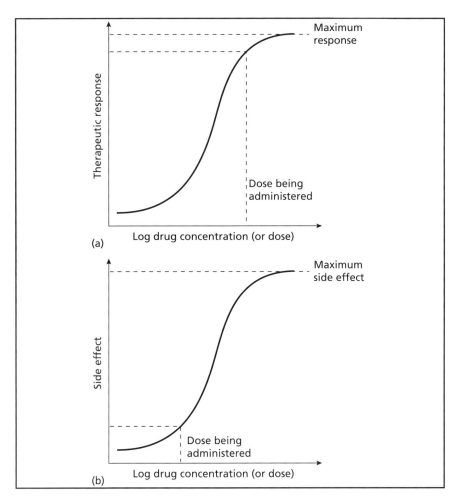

▲**Fig. 18** (**a**) Increases in drug dose may not enhance the therapeutic response, if the dose being administered already lies close to the top of the dose–response curve. (**b**) Instead, it may lead to more side effects.

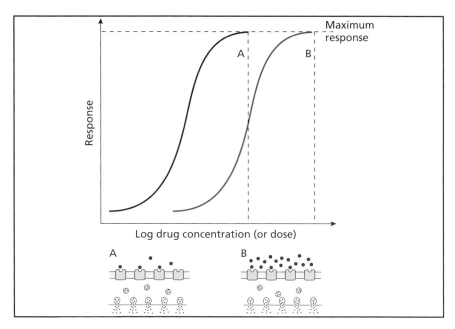

Fig. 19 A drug of lower potency (B) elicits the same maximum response as a drug of high potency (A), provided that a higher dose is used.

response as a highly potent drug, provided that it is administered at a higher dose (Fig. 19).

In clinical practice, the potency of the drug is less important than its efficacy, which refers to the maximum response that a drug elicits when all its target receptors are occupied. Some agonist drugs fail to elicit a maximal response despite maximum receptor occupancy (Fig. 20). Such drugs are called partial agonists. In the presence of a full agonist, a partial agonist can have antagonist effects because it competes with the full agonist for occupation of a receptor but fails to elicit the same degree of response.

Example 16: Addition of a new drug may have a subtractive effect

A 55-year-old man is receiving morphine subcutaneously through a continuous infusion device for postoperative analgesia after a sigmoid colectomy. Pain control is suboptimal and the patient requests sublingual buprenorphine, which he has used in the past to good effect.

Clinical approach

Both morphine and buprenorphine are opioid analgesics that target the μ-opioid receptor in the central nervous system (CNS). Morphine is a full agonist at this receptor, but buprenorphine is a partial agonist. Although an effective analgesic on its own, buprenorphine would be expected to antagonise the action of morphine and may, in this instance, worsen the pain control. The appropriate management strategy here should be to define more precisely the nature of the pain, to exclude immediately remediable causes such as a blocked urinary catheter and, if necessary, to increase the morphine dose.

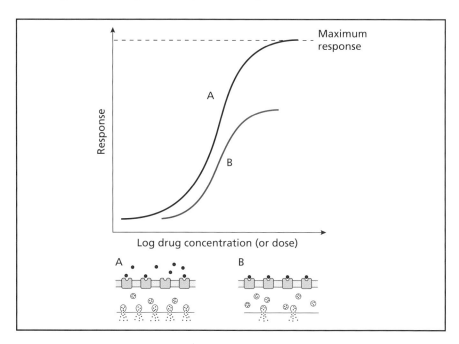

Fig. 20 Compared with the full agonist (A), the partial agonist (B) fails to elicit the maximum response despite full receptor occupancy.

Antagonists

Some drugs achieve their effect by binding and occupying a receptor without activating it. In so doing they inhibit the binding of the natural ligand to the receptor and attenuate the normal biological function. Many drugs of this type are in clinical use (see Table 13) and most are reversible competitive antagonists, meaning that their binding to the target receptor is reversible and that they compete with the natural ligand for receptor occupancy. Their effect is to increase the concentration of natural ligand required to produce a given response, so the effect of the antagonist can be overcome by

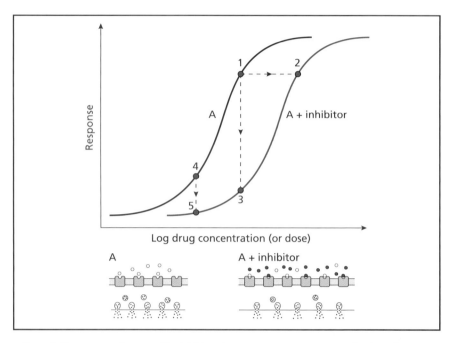

▲ **Fig. 21** In the presence of a competitive inhibitor, the concentration–response curve for the endogenous ligand A is shifted to the right. With a higher concentration of ligand A (point 1 to point 2), the effect of the inhibitor can be overcome and the same response can be attained. When a system is highly active (point 1 vs point 4), the effect of an inhibitor is greater (compare the large change in response from point 1 to point 3 with the change from point 4 to point 5).

increases in the concentration of the natural ligand (Fig. 21). Another feature of such drugs is that their effect is dependent on the degree of activation of the pathway of which the receptor is part: the more active the pathway, the greater the biological effect of the antagonist (Fig. 21).

Example 17: Too much benzodiazepine

A 79-year-old woman, recently widowed, is brought to the Emergency Department by ambulance. She is unconscious with a Glasgow Coma Scale score of 8/15, but is breathing spontaneously with a Guedel airway *in situ* and a respiratory rate of 16/minute. Her pulse rate is 80 bpm and BP 144/86 mmHg. There is no evidence of meningeal irritation and there are no focal neurological signs or signs of head injury. An empty bottle of temazepam tablets was found in her purse. Flumazenil 1 mg intravenously produces a prompt, complete but short-lived reversal of unconsciousness.

Clinical approach

This woman exhibits the features of a major benzodiazepine overdose. The CNS depressant effects of this drug can be reversed by flumazenil, which can be used to make the diagnosis of benzodiazepine overdose and exclude other toxic/metabolic causes of coma. The effects of flumazenil are short-lived because its half-life (1 hour) is much shorter than that of temazepam (about 11 hours). Sedation may return, and appropriate measures to support breathing and circulation need to be taken while the benzodiazepine is metabolised.

Flumazenil should not be used in the treatment of a benzodiazepine overdose, particularly if a mixed overdose with tricyclic antidepressants is suspected. Under these circumstances, the benzodiazepine may be helping to suppress seizure activity resulting from tricyclic overdose and flumazenil can precipitate a seizure.

Opioid overdose and naloxone

The half-life of the opioid antagonist naloxone is much shorter than that of most of the opioids encountered in overdose. Transient reversal of respiratory depression, sedation and coma by a bolus dose of naloxone may provide the patient and physician with a false sense of security, because respiratory depression may return as the naloxone is metabolised. Patients should be advised to remain under close observation and respiratory support provided if required. A continuous infusion of naloxone may be needed.

Physiological antagonism

Some agents interfere with the action of a natural ligand or another drug not by blocking its receptor but by increasing the activity of a separate system or pathway that has an opposing action. Such a process is termed 'physiological antagonism'.

The phenomenon of physiological antagonism may be used to good effect in patients who develop hypoglycaemia after overdose with insulin. This can be treated by 50 mL of 50% dextrose intravenously or, if venous access is difficult, by 1 mg glucagon by intramuscular injection. Glucagon causes glycogenolysis and the mobilisation of hepatic glucose stores that reverse the hypoglycaemia, an example of physiological antagonism.

Glucagon also finds use as a physiological antagonist in the management of severe beta-blocker overdose. The manifestations of such an overdose include bronchospasm (which can be treated by nebulised salbutamol), bradycardia (which is treated by temporary pacing or atropine, in another example of physiological antagonism) and hypotension caused by the direct negative inotropic effects of beta-blockers. In this situation glucagon, given by intravenous infusion, binds its receptors on the myocardium and increases intracellular concentrations of cyclic AMP (cyclic adenosine 3′,5′-monophosphate), thus opposing the negative inotropic effects of beta-blockers.

Inhibitors and blockers

Membrane receptors are not the only targets for drugs that interfere with a natural function. Drugs that inhibit the function of enzymes are referred to as inhibitors and drugs that inhibit the function of ion channels as blockers. Enzyme inhibition and channel blockade can also be reversible or irreversible.

A drug that inhibits an enzyme irreversibly can have biological effects that persist long after the drug is withdrawn. Examples include aspirin (whose antiplatelet effect is mediated by irreversible inhibition of cyclooxygenase) and the traditional irreversible monoamine oxidase (MAO) inhibitors, which are used as antidepressants. These drugs may need to be stopped before surgery (as aspirin can potentiate blood loss, and MAO inhibitors have adverse interactions with certain anaesthetic agents); if so, aspirin should be withdrawn about 10 days preoperatively and MAO inhibitors 2–3 weeks beforehand. A reversible inhibitor of MAO-A (eg moclobemide) can be used as an alternative antidepressant during this time.

Tolerance: why drug effects sometimes wane

The effect of a drug sometimes lessens with continued use. Tachyphylaxis, desensitisation or tolerance are terms used, sometimes interchangeably, to describe this phenomenon. The mechanisms underlying tolerance are varied and may be pharmacokinetic (the result of enhanced drug metabolism) or pharmacodynamic (the result of changes in receptor numbers or the sensitivity of postreceptor signalling mechanisms). Sometimes tolerance arises from an adaptive response of a tissue caused by the upregulation of a counter-regulatory system.

Patients receiving organic nitrates for angina develop tolerance to their effects with dose regimens that sustain plasma or tissue nitrate concentrations for more than a 24-hour period. The mechanisms underlying nitrate tolerance are unknown, but it has been suggested that depletion of tissue sulphydryl or thiol groups (necessary for the effects of nitrates), increased generation of antioxidants or reflex activation of the renin–angiotensin system may all play a part. The only measure shown to be effective in preventing nitrate tolerance is the use of a dosing schedule that gives a nitrate-free interval during some part of the day.

FURTHER READING

Ross EM and Kenakin TP. Pharmacodynamics: mechanisms of drug action and the relationship between drug concentration and effect. In: Hardman JG and Limbird LE, eds. *Goodman and Gilman's the Pharmacological Basis of Therapeutics*, 10th edn. New York: McGraw-Hill, 2001: 31–44.

3.4 Heterogeneity of drug responses, pharmacogenetics and pharmacogenomics

'One drug does not fit all.' (Andrew Marshall)

All clinicians are aware that some patients respond better to some drugs than others. This is particularly true for disorders such as hypertension, where the underlying pathophysiology is unknown and different classes of drug are often tried sequentially until an adequate therapeutic response is achieved. Just as common variation in the sequence of certain key genes (polymorphisms) can influence the way that different individuals metabolise drugs (see Table 7), so it is possible that polymorphisms in other genes might influence pharmacodynamic responses through effects on the expression or activity of receptors, ion channels or enzymes. However, there are currently few examples of the use of genetic information to guide prescribing.

Pharmacogenetics

Pharmacogenetics is the study of genetically determined variations in drug metabolism. It is clinically important because pharmacogenetic variation underlies certain adverse drug reactions, which can result in variations in response to commonly prescribed drugs and hence unexpected toxicity or therapeutic failure. An example seen in clinical practice is that of the enzyme resposible for the breakdown of azathioprine, thiopurine methyltransferase. One-tenth of whites are heterozygous for common variants in this gene, which results in inability of the enzyme to clear toxic metabolites of azathioprine. Accumulation of these metabolites can cause severe and in some cases life-threatening bone marrow suppression. It is now possible to predict which patients are more susceptible to this form of toxicity by looking for these gene alterations, and this is now done routinely in some centres.

Variants in cytochrome P450 2C9 (the enzyme that metabolises warfarin) and the vitamin K epoxide reductase complex subunit 1 enzyme (which regulates the regeneration of vitamin K) both influence the maintenance dose of warfarin required and the risk of over-anticoagulation and bleeding. Nevertheless, it is uncertain if the size of the effect is great enough to alter the current approach, particularly when set in the context of dietary and lifestyle factors, as well as drug interactions that also influence the outcome of warfarin treatment.

Pharmacogenomics

This is the term given to an emerging discipline that aims to identify the genetic determinants of pharmacodynamic responses and to use this information to guide therapy and limit side effects. It is still in its infancy and there are few examples of its utility.

An illustration of the potential importance of pharmacogenomics is provided by individuals with a common mutation in the gene for factor V (factor V Leiden), who are resistant to the fibrinolytic actions of activated protein C and at high risk of venous thromboembolic disease. In women with this mutation who are exposed to the third-generation combined oral contraceptive pill, which contains progestogens that reduce activated protein C activity, there is an interaction between these two risk factors that causes a substantial magnification of thromboembolic risk.

FURTHER READING

Rieder MJ, Reiner AP, Gage BF, *et al*. Effect of VKORC1 haplotypes on transcriptional regulation and warfarin dose. *N. Engl. J. Med.* 2005; 352: 2285–93.

– – – – – – – – – – – – – – –

Sanderson S, Emery J and Higgins J. CYP2C9 gene variants, drug dose, and bleeding risk in warfarin-treated patients: a HuGEnet systematic review and meta-analysis. *Genet. Med.* 2005; 7: 97–104.

'I do not want two diseases – one nature made, one doctor made.' (Napoleon Bonaparte)

4.1 Introduction

Some specific patient groups merit special consideration when prescribing medication. In the elderly, age-related changes in pharmacokinetics and pharmacodynamics can alter drug responses. The altered physiology of pregnancy and pathophysiology of renal or hepatic disease can also significantly affect pharmacokinetic and pharmacodynamic responses. These conditions are further sources of variation in drug response between individuals (Fig. 22). In addition, in the pregnant patient, the developing fetus may be exposed to drugs by transplacental transfer, and the breast-feeding mother may inadvertently expose the neonate to drugs via her breast milk. In such patients, we need to be even more careful than usual before we put pen to drug chart.

4.2 Prescribing and liver disease

Example 18: A man with a failing liver

A medical opinion is sought on a 46-year-old man who was admitted 5 days previously with abdominal pain. When admitted he was unkempt, smelling of alcohol, and aggressive and abusive to the nursing staff. He was icteric and had abnormal liver function tests. He was managed conservatively. His conscious level has deteriorated markedly over the last 24 hours.

Clinical approach

You are going to need to go through the full assessment and consideration of the causes of deteriorating conscious level (see *Acute Medicine*, Section 1.2.31). Of special consideration is the possibility of a drug-induced deterioration which has arisen because insufficient account has been taken of the effects of impaired liver function. Clinical assessment therefore requires full consideration of clinical and laboratory markers of liver disease in the context of his recent inpatient medication.

The hospital notes should be reviewed for previous admissions with alcoholic or other liver disease. The patient's family or GP might shed light on his premorbid state. Look carefully for stigmata of chronic liver disease, which suggest a significant metabolic problem. Look for signs of sedative drug effects, such as pinpoint pupils or respiratory depression from opioids. His liver function tests are deranged; take particular note of the clotting screen and serum albumin as indices of biosynthetic capacity. Check renal function, impairment of which will compromise other routes of drug clearance.

Review the drug and fluid balance chart in detail. The likely scenario is one of sedation as a result of a combination of regular opioid analgesia for his presenting complaint of abdominal pain together with benzodiazepines to control his agitated confusion (which may be related to alcohol withdrawal). Although excessive doses may not have been employed, these drugs (or their metabolites) may have gradually accumulated to marked sedative levels, an effect exacerbated if there is coexisting renal impairment.

When assessing a patient, always consider the possibility that the patient's clinical state may be at least partly drug induced. Always carefully review all prescribing information, both drug and total dose administered, especially if the patient falls into one of the 'special circumstances' discussed in this section.

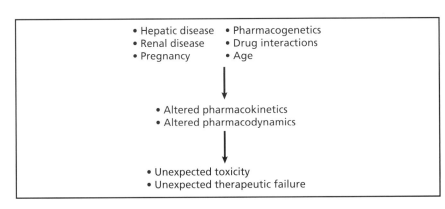

▲**Fig. 22** Some examples of sources of between-subject variability in both pharmacokinetic and pharmacodynamic responses.

TABLE 14 LIVER DISEASE MAY RESULT IN HEPATOCELLULAR DYSFUNCTION, CHOLESTASIS AND PORTOSYSTEMIC SHUNTING OF BLOOD. SUCH DYSFUNCTION RESULTS IN ALTERED PHARMACOKINETICS AND PHARMACODYNAMICS OF MANY DRUGS. SOME COMMON EXAMPLES ARE SHOWN TO ILLUSTRATE THE EFFECTS OF SUCH PATHOPHYSIOLOGY

Drug	Reason for concern
Morphine	Impaired metabolism may lead to accumulation and risk of coma Increased central nervous system (CNS) sensitivity may result in precipitation of encephalopathy
Diuretics	Can precipitate encephalopathy due to excessive potassium loss
Oral anticoagulants	Enhanced response due to reduced absorption of vitamin K in obstructive jaundice and reduced production of vitamin K-dependent clotting factors
Oral antidiabetic agents	Increased risk of hypoglycaemia with sulphonylureas Increased risk of lactic acidosis with biguanides (metformin)
Theophylline	Impaired metabolism and risk of toxicity with therapeutic dose
Clomethiazole	Marked CNS and respiratory depression due to increased sensitivity and impaired metabolism
Phenytoin	Increased risk of CNS toxicity due to reduced metabolism, especially if associated renal impairment
Lidocaine	Risk of severe CNS toxicity due to impaired metabolism and narrow therapeutic index
Vitamin D	Impaired hepatic hydroxylation of vitamin D Calcifediol (25-hydroxyvitamin D_3) is preferred
Corticosteroids	Reduced protein binding results in increased sensitivity to steroids Risk of causing fluid overload
NSAIDs	Risk of fluid overload
Carbenoxolone	Risk of fluid overload
Rifampicin	Excreted unchanged in bile; may accumulate in obstructive jaundice

General considerations

The liver performs many important metabolic functions. In the presence of significant hepatic dysfunction there may be altered pharmacodynamic responses to drugs and there are frequently clinically important changes in the pharmacokinetics of drugs that make prescribing in liver disease potentially hazardous (Table 14).

Hepatocellular dysfunction gives rise to:

- impaired drug detoxification;
- abnormal brain sensitivity;
- altered coagulation;
- low serum albumin and altered drug binding;
- risk of fluid overload.

The effect of liver disease on drug handling is not always predictable and depends on the aetiology of the disease, the stage of the illness and the degree of functional impairment. The last is difficult to predict from routinely monitored liver function tests alone. As with all adverse drug reactions, problems are most likely to arise when dealing with drugs that have a narrow therapeutic ratio and which are heavily dependent on hepatic metabolism, especially if other mechanisms of clearance are impaired.

Remember that patients with liver disease often have associated:

- renal impairment;
- cardiac impairment;
- poor nutrition;
- acute and chronic alcohol abuse;
- intravenous drug abuse;
- multiple drug therapy.

In liver disease, cholestasis may be associated with:

- failure of biliary drug excretion;
- malabsorption of vitamins and drugs.

In liver disease, portosystemic shunts give rise to:

- reduced first-pass drug metabolism;
- increased risk of gastrointestinal bleeding;
- enhanced risk of hepatic encephalopathy.

Assessment of the degree of liver dysfunction

It is difficult to make an accurate clinical assessment of the metabolic capacity of the liver and thus adjust the dosage of a drug in proportion to the changes in distribution, metabolism and pharmacodynamic responses. This results partly from the following factors.

TABLE 15 DRUG-INDUCED LIVER DAMAGE MAY OCCUR RARELY AND UNPREDICTABLY AT LOW DOSES (IDIOSYNCRATIC) OR BE A COMMON MANIFESTATION OF PROLONGED HIGH-DOSE ADMINISTRATION (DOSE DEPENDENT). THE RESULTING DAMAGE WILL BE PREDOMINANTLY LIVER CELL DAMAGE (HEPATOCELLULAR) OR INTERFERENCE WITH METABOLISM AND EXCRETION OF BILIRUBIN (CHOLESTATIC)

	Idiosyncratic	Dose dependent
Hepatocellular	General anaesthetics: halothane Antidepressants: monoamine oxidase inhibitors Antiepileptics: carbamazepine, phenytoin, phenobarbital, sodium valproate Antimicrobials: sulphonamides, isoniazid Antihypertensives: methyldopa, hydralazine	Alcohol Paracetamol Amiodarone Ketoconazole
Cholestatic	Phenothiazine neuroleptics: chlorpromazine Sulphonylureas: glibenclamide, chlorpropamide, tolbutamide Carbimazole	Sex steroids: methyltestosterone, anabolic steroids synthetic oestrogens, synthetic progestogens Antimicrobials: fusidic acid, rifampicin, erythromycin

- Hepatic function can fluctuate greatly over time.

- The liver has great reserve capacity.

- There is considerable interindividual variation in hepatic drug metabolism.

- Conventional liver function tests (alanine transaminase, alkaline phosphatase and γ-glutamyl transferase) are markers of liver cell damage rather than metabolic function.

Adjustment of drug dosage in liver disease

Unlike in renal disease, there is no simple test of liver function that enables a therapeutic regimen to be simply adjusted. The following increase the likelihood of abnormal drug handling:

- encephalopathy;
- ascites;
- abnormal coagulation;
- low serum albumin;
- jaundice.

Susceptibility of patients with liver disease to known hepatotoxic drugs

Some drugs carry risks of causing hepatic damage (Table 15). This is mainly because of the following:

- liver disease may increase the risk of some idiosyncratic hypersensitivity-type reactions;

- liver disease significantly increases the risk of dose-related reactions.

Potentially hepatotoxic drugs should be avoided or (if absolutely necessary) used in reduced dosage in patients with pre-existing liver disease because they may cause further damage to the reduced hepatic reserve; they may also confuse the management of the existing liver disease.

Drugs are frequently implicated in the aetiology of both common and rare forms of hepatic disease. Always consider the possibility of drug-induced liver disease if there are unexplained abnormalities in the routine liver function tests.

General principles of prescribing in liver disease

When prescribing for patients with liver disease bear in mind the following.

- Always perform a careful risk–benefit assessment: if benefits do not outweigh the risks, then do not prescribe.
- Select drugs with no potential for hepatotoxicity.
- Select drugs that are mainly excreted unchanged by the kidneys.
- Avoid drugs with effects on the CNS.
- Avoid drugs that affect coagulation.
- Avoid drugs that promote salt and water retention.
- Start with small doses and increase cautiously.
- Monitor levels of drug when feasible.

FURTHER READING

British National Formulary (section on prescribing for the elderly). London: BMJ Publishing Group and the Royal Pharmaceutical Society of Great Britain.

British National Formulary (Appendix 2: Liver disease). London: BMJ Publishing Group and the Royal Pharmaceutical Society of Great Britain.

James I. Prescribing in liver disease. *Br. J. Hosp. Med.* 1975; 13 (Suppl. 1): 67–76.

Rodighiero V. Effects of liver disease on pharmacokinetics: an update. *Clin. Pharmacokinet.* 1999; 37: 399–431.

4.3 Prescribing in pregnancy

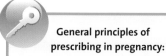

'Drugs may be administered to pregnant women, if required, from the fourth to seventh month of gestation.' (Hippocrates, 400 BC)

General principles of prescribing in pregnancy:

- Remember that although medication often has to be prescribed, 'no drug is safe beyond all doubt in early pregnancy' (*British National Formulary*).
- Safety data are generally derived from a retrospective analysis of accumulated patient exposure (controlled clinical trials would be unethical in such circumstances), so older drugs with better-known side effects are generally preferred.
- During pregnancy the mother and baby constitute a single 'maternofetal unit': the well-being of the mother is an absolute requirement for the well-being of the fetus.
- The mother should always be treated to maintain optimal health while all attempts are made to reduce the risk to the fetus (Fig. 23).

Example 19: Deep venous thrombosis in pregnancy

A 20-year-old woman presents at 10 weeks into her pregnancy with a painful swollen calf.

Clinical approach

Your main concern is that the patient has developed a deep venous thrombosis in the context of pregnancy and will thus require anticoagulation. The management of any medical condition in a pregnant woman is complicated by the potential harm any prescribed drugs may cause to the fetus, together with alteration in maternal drug handling as a consequence of the physiological changes of pregnancy. Warfarin and heparin both have particular problems associated with their use in pregnancy (Tables 16 and 17; Fig. 24).

- Warfarin: in addition to the usual bleeding risk to the mother associated with anticoagulation, warfarin readily crosses the placenta, enters the fetal circulation and poses a serious risk to the fetus.
- Heparin is a highly charged compound with high molecular weight and is thus unusual in that it does not cross the placenta. Low-molecular-weight heparins are often preferred because of convenience of administration and lack of requirement for regular monitoring of coagulation, and also because women can often be taught to self-administer these at home. The use of heparin in pregnancy

is associated with minimal risk to the fetus, but is associated with increased maternal risk. However, the fetotoxicity associated with warfarin leads most obstetricians to prefer regimens based on heparin alone (Fig. 24, Regimen 2).

Complications of prescribing during pregnancy

Drug treatment in the pregnant woman raises issues related to the well-being of both the mother and the fetus.

Fetal well-being

The main concern relates to possible transplacental transfer of drugs (Fig. 23). In general the following rules apply.

- All drugs cross the placenta unless extremely large and highly polar (eg heparin).

- The degree and rate of transfer are fastest for small, non-polar and lipid-soluble drugs.

- After a single dose of a drug, the fetus is generally exposed to a lower concentration of the drug than the mother and the time taken to achieve a peak concentration in the fetus is thus delayed.

TABLE 16 FETAL COMPLICATIONS OF WARFARIN THERAPY

Complication	Time of exposure	Manifestations	Aetiology
Warfarin embryopathy	'Critical window' of 6–9 weeks of pregnancy	Nasal hypoplasia, depression of nasal bridge, hypoplasia of extremities and stippling of epiphyses	Reduced carboxylation of calcium-binding proteins
Neurological damage	After critical window	Mental retardation, microcephaly, optic atrophy and blindness	Possibly haemorrhagic in origin, hence may be reduced by tight anticoagulant control
Haemorrhagic	During delivery	Traumatic intracranial haemorrhage during vaginal delivery	Reduced clotting factors in full-term neonate compared with older infants

Timing (weeks)	Stage	Events	Potential toxicity	Comments
2	Blastogenesis	Conception to implantation Establishment utero-placental perfusion	'All or none period' Fetus survives unharmed or early death and spontaneous abortion	Small number of pluripotent cells replace damaged cells or all cells damaged and fetus aborted Mother may experience 'late period'
2–4–6–8	Embryogenesis	Organogenesis and development of all major systems	Drug-induced fetal mal-formations	Many women still unaware that they are pregnant
38	Fetogenesis	Further growth and differentiation of major systems, esp. central nervous system	Growth retardation Intellectual impairment	Subtle effects on cognition may go undetected

▲ **Fig. 23** The risk of drug toxicity is intimately related to the stages of fetal development.

TABLE 17 MATERNAL COMPLICATIONS OF HEPARIN THERAPY

Complication	Comment
Osteoporosis	Subclinical bone demineralisation common Significant demineralisation with fractures is rare
Immune thrombocytopenia	Very rare
Maternal haemorrhage at time of delivery	Risk reduced by good anticoagulant control

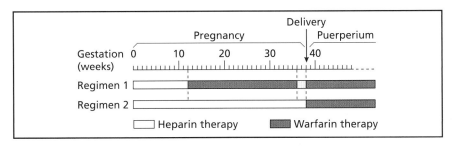

▲ **Fig. 24** Anticoagulant regimens in pregnancy.

- After repeat dosing, the fetus is generally exposed to similar steady-state concentrations as the mother.

- The nature of any fetal damage depends on the time of drug administration in relation to the stage of fetal development.

Teratogenicity

A teratogen (Greek: *teras*, monster) is a substance that causes structural or functional abnormalities in a fetus exposed to the substance (Table 18). In general, the following comments apply to teratogenicity.

- It is associated with a window of opportunity related to critical developmental activities in the target system(s), eg warfarin teratogenicity between 6 and 9 weeks of development.

- It is a dose-dependent effect.

- It is species dependent (may be non-teratogenic in some species, or affect a different system).

- The mechanism is often obscure but may be the result of specific or multifactorial effects on the embryo, or effects on the placenta or the mother.

TABLE 18 COMMONLY PRESCRIBED DRUGS THAT ARE FETOTOXIC. SOME DRUGS (EG ACE INHIBITORS) SHOULD NOT BE PRESCRIBED, WHEREAS OTHERS (EG CARBAMAZEPINE) ARE COMMONLY USED WITH CLOSE MONITORING

Drug or class	Adverse effect	Comments
ACE inhibitors and angiotensin receptor antagonists	Renal agenesis and oligohydramnios	Angiotensin is important in controlling development of the fetal kidney
Aminoglycoside antibiotics	Ototoxicity	For example, gentamicin
Carbamazepine	Increased risk of neural tube defects	Affects about 1% of pregnancies. Advise supplementation with folic acid prior to and during pregnancy, close monitoring by AFP and ultrasonography
Coumarin anticoagulants, eg warfarin	Fetal warfarin syndrome of CNS and skeletal abnormalities	About 16% of fetuses are affected, and spontaneous abortion is common (8%). Also increased risk of bleeding at term
Lithium	Increased risk of Ebstein's anomaly	Risk not known but small. Advise close ultrasound monitoring of pregnancy
Phenytoin	Fetal hydantoin syndrome with dysmorphism, CNS and skeletal defects	5–10% of fetuses have full syndrome, more have partial or intellectual impairment. Alternative agents are preferred, but if phenytoin is required for seizure control then aim for low therapeutic level and close monitoring by ultrasound scanning
Tetracycline	Staining of teeth	50% incidence if exposed after 4 weeks
Valproic acid	Spina bifida, CNS and cardiac defects	About 1% risk of neural tube defects. Monitor AFP and ultrasound scanning

ACE, angiotensin-converting enzyme; AFP, alpha-fetoprotein; CNS, central nervous system.

- The susceptibility is influenced by the genetic profile of the fetus.

- Many abnormalities that are attributed to drug treatment occur with a background frequency in the absence of the drug.

- Many disease states in pregnancy are themselves 'teratogenic'.

> All prescribing decisions have to be carefully assessed in pregnancy, but there are some circumstances that commonly cause difficulties.
> - Chronic medical problems existing before pregnancy, eg asthma or epilepsy.
> - Medical emergencies in a previously fit mother that arise during the pregnancy, eg thromboembolic disease, cardiac dysrhythmias, pre-eclampsia and infections.
> - Minor ailments related or unrelated to the pregnancy, eg nausea or back pain.

> Human teratogens are readily identified if they frequently cause dramatic but otherwise rare malformations (eg thalidomide). However, even drugs that are currently considered 'safe' during fetogenesis might cause very subtle effects, eg on cognition, that are likely to go undetected.

Complications of drug administration at term

Drugs given around the time of delivery may cause problems that arise because of one of the following:

- interference with the progress of labour;

- suppression of fetal systems after delivery, eg opioids causing respiratory depression;

- interference with cardiopulmonary physiological changes at term, eg premature closure of the ductus arteriosus;

- increased fetal and maternal bleeding during labour, eg warfarin.

Maternal well-being

The changes that occur in maternal physiology during pregnancy result in changes in drug handling by the body (pharmacokinetics). In general (but not always) these tend to reduce the plasma levels of an active drug compared with the non-pregnant state. Alterations in the pharmacokinetics of drugs in pregnancy can lead to unexpected toxicity or therapeutic failure at doses used in non-pregnant women. It is particularly important to monitor plasma levels of those compounds with a narrow therapeutic window whenever possible, eg digoxin and lithium (Table 19).

TABLE 19 CHANGES IN PHYSIOLOGY AS A RESULT OF PREGNANCY CAN ALTER DRUG HANDLING. THIS CAN BE SIGNIFICANT FOR A FEW COMMON DRUGS AND NECESSITATE CHANGES IN DOSE DURING PREGNANCY

Drug	Change in therapeutic effect	Mechanism	Comments
Lithium	Reduced	Increased renal clearance	Clearance doubles during pregnancy and significant dose increases may be required. Levels can rise rapidly after delivery if dose not reduced to pre-pregnancy levels
Digoxin	Reduced	Increased renal clearance	May require twice the non-pregnant dose towards end of pregnancy
Phenytoin	Variable	Increased hepatic metabolism, reduced absorption and reduced plasma protein binding	Reduced plasma protein binding offsets the reduction in absorption and increase in metabolism
Penicillins	Reduced	Increased renal clearance	Half the expected plasma levels may be obtained at end of pregnancy

Alterations in maternal drug handling may arise because of a number of physiological changes that occur in pregnancy:

- increased volume of distribution as a result of increase in total body water;
- altered drug absorption;
- reduced plasma protein binding;
- increased hepatic drug metabolism;
- increased renal clearance.

The restoration of non-pregnant physiology after delivery can result in rapid accumulation of drugs, the dose of which have been increased to maintain adequate levels towards the end of pregnancy. Early restoration of the pre-pregnancy dose is required to prevent digoxin or lithium toxicity in the puerperium.

4.4 Prescribing for women of childbearing potential

You should remember that any woman of childbearing potential may be pregnant (and unaware of the fact) or may become pregnant subsequently.

When prescribing for any woman of childbearing potential it is important to:

- exclude pregnancy if prescribing a drug that might pose a known teratogenic risk;
- determine whether the patient is attempting to become pregnant or at risk of an unplanned pregnancy;
- consider whether the prescribed drug might interfere with hormonal methods of contraception.

Before prescribing:

- check if the drug can cause fetal damage;
- clearly inform the patient of the potential risks of using or withholding such a drug, so that she can make informed decisions regarding treatment and pregnancy, and document your discussion in the case notes.

FURTHER READING

British National Formulary (Appendix 4: Pregnancy). London: BMJ Publishing Group and the Royal Pharmaceutical Society of Great Britain.

– – – – – – – – – – – – – – – – –

Rubin P, ed. *Prescribing in Pregnancy*, 3rd edn. London: BMJ Books, 2000.

– – – – – – – – – – – – – – – – –

UK National Teratology Information Service, Regional Drug and Therapeutics Centre, Newcastle. For contact details see website at http://www.nyrdtc.nhs.uk/Services/teratology/teratology.html

4.5 Prescribing to lactating mothers

Example 20: Breast is best, but there can be problems

A 32-year-old nurse needed treatment for pregnancy-induced hypertension with methyldopa. This is her second child and the previous pregnancy was complicated by quite severe postnatal depression. Her BP remains elevated post delivery and it is considered that she should stay on treatment. She intends to breast-feed and is concerned about passing any medication on to her baby.

Clinical approach

As with prescribing in pregnancy, most information on the safety of drugs in breast-feeding relates to older agents. Most drugs are passed into breast milk to some extent and thence to the neonate, but usually this does not constitute a significant problem. It would be possible to continue methyldopa therapy because this is present in breast milk in amounts that are too small to be harmful. However, methyldopa is known to cause sedation and to increase the likelihood of a depressive episode, and given the history of severe postnatal depression continued use of this agent would not be advisable.

Most of the more modern antihypertensives are excreted to a variable extent in breast milk and the manufacturers generally advise against their use in a breast-feeding mother. However, the mother can be reassured that satisfactory management of her hypertension can be achieved without the necessity of stopping breast-feeding: a suitable agent can be selected after discussion with the mother and reference to published advice regarding the safety of drugs in breast-feeding.

General considerations

In general, all drugs given to a breast-feeding mother will enter her breast milk, but most drugs are not selectively excreted in it and hence exposure of the neonate will usually be considerably below that of the mother. However, some drugs may be concentrated in specific organs and exaggerated pharmacokinetic or pharmacodynamic responses may be seen as a result of differences in fetal physiology, especially in preterm babies (Table 20).

Drugs administered to the mother may suppress lactation and mothers must be fully informed of any risk to their likely ability to continue to breast-feed. Drugs that cause sedation in the adult may do so in the neonate and this may impair suckling.

Classification of drugs administered to the breast-feeding mother

In broad terms, drugs that might be used in breast-feeding mothers may be divided into three categories as follows.

1. Drugs known to produce specific problems and which are contraindicated or should be used only with caution. If such agents are required for maternal well-being, the mother will almost certainly need to bottle-feed (Table 21).

2. Drugs that can be administered because they appear in amounts in the milk that are too small to be harmful to the neonate.

3. Drugs not known to be harmful to the neonate, although they are present in significant quantities in breast milk.

TABLE 20 THE NEONATE MAY SHOW INCREASED SENSITIVITY TO DRUGS EXCRETED IN BREAST MILK AS A RESULT OF ALTERED PHAMACOKINETICS OR PHARMACODYNAMICS

Change	Mechanism	Effect
Pharmacokinetic	Absorption	Generally unaffected
	Hepatic metabolism	Reduced albumin biosynthesis
		Reduced clotting factor synthesis
		Reduced enzymic drug metabolism
	Renal excretion	Relatively low GFR
Pharmacodynamic	–	Increased sensitivity to respiratory depressant action of morphine

GFR, glomerular filtration rate.

TABLE 21 A NUMBER OF DRUGS ARE ASSOCIATED WITH PROBLEMS IN MOTHERS WHO ARE BREAST-FEEDING AND SHOULD BE AVOIDED

Drug	Comments
Cytotoxics	Inherent toxicity
Radioiodine	Concentrated in the milk with a milk/plasma ratio of 70:1 Further concentrated in the fetal thyroid gland Subsequent increase in risk of permanent hypothyroidism and thyroid cancer
Bromocriptine	Suppresses lactation
Chloramphenicol	Aplastic anaemia (grey baby syndrome) due to low glucuronyl transferase activity
Aspirin	Association with Reye's syndrome
Dothiepin	Sedation and respiratory depression due to active metabolite
Laxatives	Increased gastric motility and diarrhoea
Antipsychotics	Animal studies suggest potential adverse effects on development of the central nervous system
Antiepileptics	Some agents may cause sedation
Theophylline	Slow clearance with irritability and possible sleep disturbance

For most drugs there is inadequate evidence to provide reliable guidance on their safety in breast-feeding. As with pregnancy, it is best to administer only those drugs that are considered necessary for maternal well-being.

FURTHER READING

British National Formulary (Appendix 5: Breast-feeding). London: BMJ Publishing Group and the Royal Pharmaceutical Society of Great Britain.

4.6 Prescribing in renal disease

Example 21: Doing well, but then 'went off'

You are contacted by a junior medical colleague who is getting to know her new patients. She is alarmed by the state of a 70-year-old woman who has been an inpatient for 3 weeks on an outlying ward following repair of a fractured neck of femur. Initially she did well postoperatively, apart from an episode of apparent heart failure, but she has gradually become unwell, with confusion and drowsiness. Her renal function, last checked 2 weeks ago, showed a creatinine of 180 μmol/L and a urea of 15 mmol/L; her blood tests today reveal a creatinine of 700 μmol/L and a urea of 52 mmol/L. The junior medical colleague attributes the deterioration to adverse effects of drugs (shown in Table 22).

Clinical approach

The first priority is to exclude hyperkalaemia, a life-threatening complication of renal failure. This is not present in this case and the house officer is correct in her assessment. One week after surgery the woman clearly had significant renal impairment, which could have been acute (precipitated by the immediate effects of hip fracture or surgery) or chronic, and her drug treatment is very likely to have induced further acute deterioration in renal function as follows.

- Laxative and diuretic therapy might have resulted in underfilling of the circulation, at a time when the renin–angiotensin system is activated and glomerular filtration is critically dependent on afferent and efferent glomerular arteriolar tone.
- NSAID: blockade of afferent glomerular arteriolar dilatation (as a result partly of vasodilator prostaglandins) may reduce glomerular filtration, making dependence on the activated renin–angiotensin system even more critical.

- Angiotensin-converting enzyme (ACE) inhibitor: prevention of angiotensin II production leads to reduction in efferent arteriolar tone, the final straw for this woman's renal function.

The episode of 'heart failure' may have been caused by excessive fluid administration in the immediate postoperative period or may have resulted from pre-existing cardiac disease, thereby further contributing to underperfusion of the kidneys and predisposing to acute-on-chronic renal failure.

The patient's clinical deterioration is a result of uraemia exacerbated by the retention of, and increased sensitivity to, the opioid analgesic contained in the compound preparation co-codamol. Management requires removal of the drugs contributing to nephrotoxicity, careful restoration of circulatory volume and withdrawal of opioid analgesics. Naloxone could be administered if the clinical state warrants this.

How could the problem have been avoided?

The electrolytes and renal function tests should have been much more closely monitored.

The kidney is the major site of drug excretion: renal impairment is therefore associated with significant alterations in the pharmacokinetic parameters of many drugs (Table 23). Renal disease may also be associated with altered pharmacodynamic responses that may be:

- enhanced, eg increased sensitivity to sedative drugs or antiplatelet agents;
- reduced, eg reduced sensitivity to diuretics.

Many drugs can exacerbate renal impairment, which is not always reversible.

	Drug	Dosage
TABLE 22 DRUGS PRESCRIBED BEFORE ADMISSION AND CONTINUED DURING ADMISSION		
Drugs prescribed before admission and continued during admission	Furosemide	80 mg once daily (recently increased from 40 mg)
	Quinine sulphate	300 mg at night
	Ibuprofen	500 mg twice daily
	Co-danthramer	10 mL twice daily
Additional drugs prescribed during admission	Lisinopril	10 mg once daily
	Co-codamol	Two tablets four times daily as needed
	Prochlorperazine	10 mg three times daily as needed

TABLE 23 REDUCED GLOMERULAR FILTRATION IS THE PRIMARY CONCERN WITH REGARDS TO ABNORMAL DRUG HANDLING IN RENAL FAILURE. OTHER MECHANISMS CAN CONTRIBUTE TO ALTERED DRUG RESPONSES

Abnormality	Effect	Mechanism
Pharmacokinetic Primary importance	Reduced renal clearance	Reduced glomerular filtration Reduced tubular secretion
Secondary considerations	Reduced drug absorption	Increased gastric pH Binding of drugs to phosphate-binding agents
	Reduced protein binding	Acidosis Low serum albumin
	Drug volume of distribution may be altered	
Pharmacodynamic	Increased sensitivity	Central nervous system depressants Hypotensives or fluid-retaining drugs according to fluid balance Anticoagulants Neostigmine (reduced cholinesterase activity)

Problems with toxicity are most likely to occur with drugs that have a narrow therapeutic window and are highly dependent on renal excretion for clearance (eg digoxin, aminoglycosides, lithium). The doses of such drugs, which are excreted by the kidney as a parent compound or active metabolite, may need to be modified depending on laboratory estimates of the degree of renal impairment. The plasma concentration of some drugs may be monitored (eg digoxin, lithium, aminoglycosides, ciclosporin). Always consider the contribution of dialysis to drug clearance in patients on renal replacement therapy.

Furosemide in renal failure

There are two main pathways of tubular secretion that affect weak organic acids and weak organic bases (see Fig. 10). The organic acids that accumulate in renal failure compete with drugs that are normally secreted via this route. One such drug is furosemide, which must enter the tubular lumen to act. Therefore, much higher doses need to be given to patients with renal impairment, partly to overcome the competition from organic acids that block its tubular secretion.

Assessment of the severity of renal impairment

The serum creatinine is determined by the muscle mass of the patient and his or her renal function. Thus a 'normal' value of serum creatinine (say 100 µmol/L) indicates very different renal function in a muscular young man with a glomerular filtration rate (GFR) of perhaps 100 mL/min compared with that in an old woman with a GFR of perhaps 30 mL/min. A more precise estimate of GFR can be obtained by measurement or estimation of creatinine clearance.

Measurement of creatinine clearance requires a 24-hour urinary collection, which is cumbersome and often performed inaccurately. Therefore the usual method for estimating GFR (eGFR) in clinical practice is to perform a calculation based on one of many formulae that take into account the patient's serum creatinine, age, sex and (sometimes) weight and/or race. The most widely used is the abbreviated Modification of Diet in Renal Disease (MDRD) equation which, in the form typically used by clinical chemistry laboratories, reports eGFR based on the patient's serum creatinine, age and sex, with the standing instruction that the value should be multiplied by 1.21 if the patient is of black race (to account for their higher muscle mass). Many laboratories now routinely report eGFR in conjunction with any measurement of serum creatinine made in a non-acute setting and report chronic kidney disease (CKD) stages as follows.

- CKD1: eGFR >90 mL/min, in a patient with other evidence of renal disease.

- CKD2: eGFR 60–90 mL/min, in a patient with other evidence of renal disease.

- CKD3: eGFR 30–60 mL/min.

- CKD4: eGFR 15–30 mL/min.

- CKD5: eGFR <15 mL/min.

When considering eGFR as derived by the abbreviated MDRD equation it is important to recognise the following.

- It is an estimate and not a precise value, eg it will be inaccurate in people with extreme body types, underestimating true GFR in those with big muscles and overestimating true GFR in those with little muscle.

TABLE 24 THE CREATININE CLEARANCE CAN BE ESTIMATED FROM THE SERUM CREATININE. THE SEVERITY OF RENAL IMPAIRMENT CAN THEN BE DETERMINED AND ALTERED DOSING REGIMENS IMPLEMENTED

Grade	Creatinine clearance (GFR) (mL/min)	CKD stage
Mild	20–50	3/4
Moderate	10–20	4/5
Severe	<10	5

- The creatinine level must be stable: eGFR calculations are not valid if serum creatinine is changing.

- It is not valid in pregnant women or children (<18 years old).

Renal impairment may be divided arbitrarily into three grades, which correspond to those used by the pharmaceutical industry in the product-labelling information provided with all medications for the purposes of prescribing (Table 24).

Plasma creatinine will be normal (for a short time) even if there is no glomerular filtration! In acute renal failure creatinine will be accumulating rapidly in the plasma, but this cannot be discerned from a single value. GFR can be predicted only if the plasma creatinine is stable.

Adjustment of drug dosage in renal impairment

The clinical development of new drugs includes studies specifically conducted in patients with impaired renal function in order to provide data on alterations in pharmacokinetics and pharmacodynamics. The half-life of drugs excreted in an active form by the kidney will be prolonged in renal impairment if the dosage is not modified. The degree of renal impairment that necessitates a dose adjustment will depend on:

- alternative clearance mechanisms available for the drug;
- the degree of toxicity of the drug.

An adjustment of the initial or loading dose is not usually necessary because the volume of distribution for the drug is generally similar for uraemic and healthy subjects. Subsequent doses should be based on the severity of renal impairment and involve either:

- usual maintenance doses given less frequently;
- a lower maintenance dose given at the same frequency as in the healthy subject.

The time taken to reach steady-state concentrations is dependent only on the drug half-life. Prolongation of the half-life in renal disease will delay the time taken to reach steady-state concentrations.

Renal function may continue to deteriorate with time and further alterations in the drug regimen may be required. In the face of changing renal function, it is important to monitor patients carefully for signs of drug toxicity, either by using pharmacodynamic outcomes (eg blood sugar in patients receiving sulphonylureas or pulse rate in patients receiving atenolol) or, when appropriate, using drug plasma concentration measurements.

When faced with prescribing for a patient with renal impairment, do the following.

- First check if a dosage reduction is indicated from a standard reference such as the *British National Formulary* (Appendix 3: Renal impairment).
- The data sheet provided with the drug should indicate appropriate dose alterations according to the severity of renal impairment; alternatively, use a standard reference such as *Avery's Drug Treatment* (Appendix D: Guide to Drug Dosage in Renal Failure).

Nephrotoxic drugs

Many drugs can contribute to an acute (Table 25) or chronic (Table 26) and reversible or irreversible deterioration in renal function. The kidneys are particularly susceptible to the toxic effects of drugs because they receive a high cardiac output and have a commensurately high metabolic activity. The kidneys are the final common pathway for the excretion of many drugs and toxic metabolites, and the effects of such toxicity are likely to be more severe in the face of chronic diminished renal reserve.

Nephrotoxic drugs should be avoided if possible in patients with renal disease.

FURTHER READING

British National Formulary (Appendix 3: Renal impairment). London: BMJ Publishing Group and the Royal Pharmaceutical Society of Great Britain.

Speight TM and Holford NHG, eds. *Avery's Drug Treatment: A Guide to the Properties, Choice, Therapeutic Use and Economic Value of Drugs in Disease Management*, 4th edn. Auckland: Adis International, 1997.

TABLE 25 MECHANISMS BY WHICH DRUGS CAN CAUSE AN ACUTE DETERIORATION IN RENAL FUNCTION

	Mechanism	Example
Pre-renal	Excessive water and electrolyte loss	Diuretics and laxatives
	Increased afferent arteriolar tone	NSAIDs, ciclosporin
	Reduced efferent arteriolar tone	ACE inhibitors
	Hypercatabolism	Tetracyclines
Renal	Acute tubular necrosis resulting from direct tubular damage (especially proximal)	Aminoglycosides
		Vancomycin
		Amphotericin B
		Cefaloridine
		Radiocontrast agents
		Ciclosporin
		Cisplatin (and other anticancer agents)
		Paracetamol overdosage (mechanism as for hepatotoxicity)
	Acute interstitial nephritis	Penicillins
		NSAIDs
		Thiazide diuretics
'Post-renal'	Deposition of drug or metabolite in renal tubule with secondary damage to tubular cells	Sulphonamides
		Cytotoxics due to urate deposition
		Aciclovir
		Methotrexate
	Induction of formation of renal calculi	Vitamin D and calcium supplements

ACE, angiotensin-converting enzyme.

TABLE 26 DRUGS COMMONLY IMPLICATED IN CONTRIBUTING TO CHRONIC DECLINE IN RENAL FUNCTION

Mechanism	Types of agent	Examples
Direct toxicity	Immunosuppressants	Ciclosporin
	Cytotoxics	Cisplatin
	Analgesics	NSAIDs
Indirect toxicity	Cytotoxics	Urate toxicity
	Uricosurics	Urate toxicity
	Vitamin D	Hypercalcaemia

4.7 Prescribing in the elderly

'All diseases run into one, old age.' (Ralph Waldo Emerson)

General principles of prescribing in the elderly

- Elderly people often have multiple pathologies requiring multiple drug therapies, so the potential for drug interactions is great.
- Drug absorption, distribution, metabolism and elimination may be different in elderly patients and dose adjustments may be necessary.

- Elderly people may have altered pharmacodynamic responses to drugs.
- Compliance may be poor in elderly patients due to lack of understanding, poor eyesight, poor ability to open drug packaging or memory problems; aids to compliance such as dosette boxes may be helpful.
- Many elderly people take herbal and over-the-counter remedies in addition to their prescribed medication. Always take a full drug history and check for any interactions.

The incidence of adverse drug reactions is higher in the elderly due to the increased number of medications being taken, drug interactions, altered pharmacokinetic and pharmacodynamic responses, and poor compliance with dosing regimens. When prescribing for the elderly, it is important to assess whether the addition of a new drug is really necessary or whether non-pharmacological measures may be adequate. You must also regularly review whether any drugs should be withdrawn, particularly if they are ineffective or causing side effects. However, at the same time it is important to ensure that the underprescribing of medications that may be of benefit to elderly people does not occur, eg anticoagulants or antiplatelet agents in atrial fibrillation, statins and antihypertensive agents.

Altered pharmacokinetics in the elderly

Absorption

Drug absorption following oral administration may be reduced due to decreased gastrointestinal blood flow and motility along with increased gastric pH in the elderly.

However, these changes are rarely significant to cause problems with the efficacy of drugs and often affect the rate more than the extent of absorption. Drug absorption from intramuscular injection sites may be reduced due to lower muscle blood flow and reduced muscle contractions in the elderly.

Distribution

Total body water is lower in elderly people and this can affect the volume of distribution and clearance of drugs, particularly those that are water soluble. Lean body mass tends to be lower in elderly people and therefore standard doses may increase the amount of drug per unit body weight. In addition, elderly people with chronic disease may have lower levels of plasma proteins and this may affect the plasma protein binding of drugs and increase the free fraction of a drug in the plasma.

Metabolism

Liver mass and liver blood flow are significantly reduced in the elderly. This may particularly affect the clearance of drugs with a high hepatic extraction ratio, eg propranolol or lidocaine. Hepatic drug-metabolising enzymes are also slightly impaired in the elderly (particularly phase I metabolism),

although this does not cause a major problem with most drugs.

Elimination

Glomerular filtration rate decreases steadily with increasing age and may be low in the elderly despite a normal serum creatinine (due to reduced muscle mass). Tubular secretion of drugs and renal blood flow also tend to decrease with age. These changes may cause the accumulation of drugs that are largely excreted via the kidneys, such as digoxin, lithium and aminoglycosides. Doses of such agents should be reduced in the elderly.

Altered pharmacodynamics in the elderly

Elderly people are likely to show an exaggerated response to drugs acting on the central nervous system and this is particularly apparent with sedative and hypnotic drugs, which may cause prolonged drowsiness or hangover effects. Elderly people are also more sensitive to the effects of antihypertensive agents, which may cause postural hypotension, although this is partly due to reduced carotid baroreceptor sensitivity and an inability to compensate for drug-induced drops in BP.

Compliance in the elderly

Many studies have shown that compliance (adherence or concordance) with drug therapy is poorer in older people. There are several possible reasons for this. Simplification of drug regimens, careful provision of drug information, special drug packaging that is easy to open and memory aids such as timers or dosette boxes may improve compliance.

Reasons for poor compliance with drug therapy in the elderly

- Large number of prescribed drugs.
- Complicated dosing regimens.
- Actual or perceived side effects of medications.
- Insufficient information given to the patient by the prescriber.
- Poor understanding of information (hearing or visual difficulties may affect ability to absorb information).
- Lack of supportive network of family or friends.
- Poor memory.
- Poor manual dexterity and inability to open drug packaging.

FURTHER READING

Williams CM. Using medications appropriately in older adults. *Am. Fam. Physician* 2002; 66: 1917–24.

5.1 Introduction and definition

> 'Medicine is a collection of uncertain prescriptions . . . the results of which, collectively taken, are more fatal than useful to mankind. (Napoleon Bonaparte)

Adverse drug reactions are common. A UK study found that 6.5% of all acute medical admissions to hospital were related to adverse effects of drugs (not including deliberate self-harm or accidental overdose), with the adverse reaction being the direct cause of admission in 80% of these cases. Up to 20% of all hospital inpatients are subject to significant drug-related illness, and in half of these their period of stay in hospital will be prolonged as a result. In the USA, it has been calculated that one in seven of all hospital beds are taken up for the treatment of adverse reactions resulting from drugs. The morbidity, mortality and cost of drug-related disease are therefore considerable.

Definition

The definition and classification of adverse drug reactions is being constantly revised. In 1972 the World Health Organisation defined an adverse drug reaction as 'a response to a drug that is noxious and unintended and occurs at doses normally used in man for the prophylaxis, diagnosis or therapy of disease, or for modification of physiological function'. More recent definitions have modified this to include substances not traditionally regarded as drugs (such as herbal remedies) and have attempted to consider the severity of a reaction that should be described as adverse.

> **Adverse drug reaction**
>
> ". . . an appreciably harmful or unpleasant reaction, resulting from an intervention related to the use of a medicinal product, which predicts hazard from future administration and warrants prevention or specific treatment, or alteration of the dosage regimen, or withdrawal of the product.' (I.R. Edwards and J.K. Aronson)

Most definitions exclude adverse reactions arising from the administration (intentionally or otherwise) of doses greater than those normally used therapeutically (for discussion of poisoning and drug overdose, see Section 5.9 and *Acute Medicine*, Section 2.1).

'Side' effects (resulting from a pharmacological action different from the therapeutic pharmacological effect, eg bronchospasm caused by beta-blockers in the treatment of hypertension) and toxic effects (resulting from an enhanced level of the therapeutic effect, eg over-anticoagulation with anticoagulants) can both be considered adverse drug reactions.

Drug interactions are an important cause of adverse effects of drugs, and co-prescriptions should always be checked when an adverse drug reaction is suspected. There is an increasing range of therapeutically valuable drugs available in modern clinical practice and patients are increasingly taking a large number of drugs, making the potential for adverse reactions and interactions almost unlimited. Problems of polypharmacy are particularly important in the elderly, and in any situation where concordance with prescriptions is questionable.

> If you are not absolutely familiar with a drug and its potential adverse effects and interactions, LOOK IT UP.

FURTHER READING

Davies DM, Ferner RE and De Glanville H, eds. *Davies's Textbook of Adverse Drug Reactions*, 5th edn. London: Chapman & Hall, 1998.

- - - - - - - - - - - - - - - -

Dukes MNG and Aronson JK, eds. *Meyler's Side Effects of Drugs: An Encyclopedia of Adverse Reactions and Interactions*, 14th edn. Amsterdam: Elsevier, 2000.

- - - - - - - - - - - - - - - -

Pirmohamed M, James S, Meakin S, *et al.* Adverse drug reactions as a cause of admission to hospital: prospective analysis of 18,820 patients. *BMJ* 2004; 329: 15–19.

5.2 Classification of adverse drug reactions

Classification is important for identifying, managing and

avoiding adverse drug reactions. It is also a prerequisite for accurate monitoring and reporting (pharmacovigilance, see Section 6). Four broad categories of adverse drug reactions were traditionally considered:

- type A reactions (dose related);
- type B reactions (dose independent or idiosyncratic);
- type C reactions (chronic effects);
- type D reactions (delayed effects).

These categories were later expanded to six by including:

- type E reactions (end of use or withdrawal reactions);
- type F reactions (unexpected failure of therapy).

Table 27 gives details of these various types of adverse drug reactions.

More recently, an alternative three-dimensional classification that takes into account not only dose and timing in relation to an adverse drug reaction but also patient susceptibility has been proposed (DoTS: dose, time, susceptibility). Dose-related reactions in this system are considered as:

- toxic reactions that occur at supratherapeutic doses;
- collateral reactions that occur at standard therapeutic doses, ie 'side' effects;
- hypersusceptibility reactions occurring at subtherapeutic doses in susceptible patients, eg penicillin hypersensitivity.

Reactions are either time independent, rapid, first-dose, early, intermediate, late or delayed. Susceptibility is a more complex construct depending on several patient factors, but has important implications for avoidance of adverse drug reactions.

It is useful in clinical practice to identify those situations where there is a higher risk of an adverse effect, and take it into account when making prescribing decisions.

Patient factors predisposing to adverse drug reactions

- Age: adverse reactions are more common at the extremes of age.
- Sex: women are at greater risk.
- Race: pharmacogenetic variations form the basis for many adverse reactions.
- History of atopy or allergic disorders.
- History of a previous adverse drug reaction.
- Renal impairment.
- Hepatic impairment.
- Heart failure.
- Thyroid disease: both hypothyroidism and hyperthyroidism can affect the metabolism of drugs.
- Nutritional status: the overweight and undernourished are at greater risk.
- Multiple drug therapy.

5.3 Clinical approach to adverse drug reactions

Recognition and diagnosis

Adverse drug reactions may present in a variety of ways not necessarily related to the mechanism underlying the reaction (Table 28). Familiarity with common adverse reactions and pattern recognition are important, but will not detect new or less common reactions. A systematic approach when a drug reaction is suspected can help.

- Always consider an adverse drug reaction as a possible cause of a patient's symptoms. Take a careful history, remembering to ask about non-prescription medications and relating symptoms to the timing of the dose of the drug, changes in dosage or co-prescription. Are there factors that would make the patient particularly susceptible to an adverse reaction?

- Examination should focus on vital signs if a severe hypersensitivity

TABLE 27 FEATURES OF ADVERSE DRUG REACTION

Type of reaction	Features	Example
A (dose related)	Predictable Common Often seen with drugs with narrow therapeutic index Often due to pharmacokinetic or pharmacodynamic variation	Haemorrhage due to anticoagulants
B (non-dose related)	Unpredictable Immunologically mediated or genetically determined	Penicillin hypersensitivity Apnoea with suxamethonium
C (chronic)	Specific effects associated with chronicity of administration Related to cumulative dose	Long-term complications of corticosteroid therapy
D (delayed)	Uncommon Presents after use of the drug	Teratogenesis
E (withdrawal)	Reactions appearing after stopping a drug	Benzodiazepine withdrawal
F (failure)	Unexpected failure Common Often due to drug interactions	Oral contraceptive pill with enzyme inducers, eg rifampicin

TABLE 28 COMMON CLINICAL PRESENTATIONS OF ADVERSE DRUG REACTIONS

Presentation	Example	Causal Drug
Fever		
Anaphylaxis		
Rash	Urticaria and angioedema	Opioids and penicillins
	Erythema multiforme and Stevens–Johnson syndrome	Penicillins and sulphonamides
	Erythema nodosum	Sulphonamides and oral contraceptive pill
	Exfoliative dermatitis	Carbamazepine
	Purpura	Corticosteroids
Respiratory	Respiratory depression	Opioids
	Asthma	β-blockers
	Pneumonitis, fibrosis and eosinophilia	Amiodarone, nitrofurantoin, sulfasalazine and bleomycin
Blood dyscrasias	Thrombocytopenia	Heparin, thrombocytopaenia and rifampicin
	Granulocytopenia	Clozapine and carbimazole
	Aplastic anaemia	Chloramphenicol and sulphonamides
	Haemolysis	Methyldopa, penicillins, quinine and lead
Connective tissue disease	Systemic lupus erythematosus-like syndrome	Hydralazine, procainamide and isoniazid
	Hepatitis	Halothane, isoniazid, hydroxymethylglutaryl co-reductase inhibitors
	Renal dysfunction	NSAIDs, paracetamol, phenacetin, aminoglycosides and ciclosporin
	Neuropsychiatric	Tardive dyskinesia with neuroleptics Seizures with ciprofloxacin and imipenem

The most important time for monitoring adverse drug reactions is not during clinical trials done prior to licensing but in the period following licensing when many more patients, with more varying characteristics, will be exposed to the drug.

> Post-marketing surveillance is an essential tool in detecting and monitoring adverse drug reactions. Many drugs have been withdrawn on the basis of data collected in this way.

FURTHER READING

Aronson JK and Ferner RE. Joining the DoTS: new approach to classifying adverse drug reactions. *BMJ* 2003; 327: 1222–5.

Bennett PN and Brown MJ, eds. *Clinical Pharmacology*, 9th edn. Edinburgh: Churchill Livingstone, 2003.

Edwards IR and Aronson JK. Adverse drug reactions: definitions, diagnosis and management. *Lancet* 2000; 356: 1255–9.

Grahame-Smith DG and Aronson JK. *Oxford Textbook of Clinical Pharmacology and Drug Therapy*, 3rd edn. Oxford: Oxford University Press, 2002.

reaction is suspected, with special attention to skin and respiratory, gastrointestinal and hepatic systems.

Management and reporting

Severe anaphylactic reactions require rapid assessment and treatment with parenteral epinephrine, antihistamines, steroids and maximal supportive care (see *Acute Medicine*, Section 1.2.33, and *Rheumatology and Clinical Immunology*, Section 1.4.2). For less severe reactions, withdrawal of the suspected medicines followed by careful observation of the patient to confirm resolution of the symptoms may be all that is required. The nature and mechanism of the reaction will determine whether the drug can be reintroduced

on resolution of the reaction. Alternative medicines for the initial complaint may be necessary, or dose adjustments may be made to the original drug on its reintroduction.

All suspected drug reactions should be reported to the appropriate monitoring organisation. In the UK this is the Committee on Safety of Medicines, using the 'yellow card' system.

> Even when uncertain of the causal link, if there is any suspicion that a drug may have caused a serious or unexpected adverse event in a patient, then report it using the yellow cards found in the back of the *British National Formulary*.

5.4 Dose-related adverse drug reactions (type A)

> Dose-related adverse drug reactions are the commonest type of adverse drug reaction, perhaps accounting for 80% of clinically significant cases. They are largely predictable and should therefore be largely preventable.

Dose-related adverse drug reactions arise from an exaggeration of the intended therapeutic effects of a drug and are most commonly seen with drugs that have a narrow therapeutic range (see Fig. 9). They occur mainly because of pharmacokinetic or pharmacodynamic variability, both within and between individuals.

'Poisons and medicine are oftentimes the same substance given with different intents.' (Peter Mere Latham).

Example 22: A cause of confusion

A 79-year-old woman with type 2 (non-insulin-dependent) diabetes and taking glibenclamide 10 mg daily is failing to cope at home and has fallen several times. Initially this was attributed to a urinary infection, treated by her GP with trimethoprim, but now she has become acutely confused and on admission is found to have a blood glucose level of 2.1 mmol/L.

Clinical approach

The cause of this woman's falls and recent confusion was thought to be hypoglycaemia. Why has her normally good glycaemic control on a stable dose of glibenclamide recently become problematic? Glibenclamide undergoes hepatic metabolism and its active metabolites are renally excreted. Hence, in patients with renal impairment the effect of glibenclamide is exaggerated. In this case the patient developed a moderate degree of renal impairment with a creatinine of 195 μmol/L and the steady accumulation of her sulphonylurea led to symptomatic hypoglycaemia. In addition to this, there is an interaction between trimethoprim and glibenclamide that can result in an enhanced

hypoglycaemic effect. Avoid long-acting drugs that can accumulate in renal failure, such as chlorpropamide and glibenclamide. Consider instead drugs with a short half-life and that undergo a significant degree of hepatic elimination, eg glipizide.

Examples of dose-related adverse drug reactions

Excess of the intended therapeutic action (ie 'toxic' effects):

- Hypoglycaemia caused by sulphonylureas.
- Hypotension caused by vasodilator drugs.
- Dehydration caused by diuretics.
- Symptomatic bradycardia caused by beta-blockers.
- Haemorrhage caused by anticoagulants.
- Hypothyroidism caused by antithyroid drugs.

Reactions unrelated to the desired therapeutic effect (ie collateral or 'side' effects):

- Gout caused by thiazide diuretics.
- Anticholinergic effects of tricyclic antidepressants.
- Ototoxicity of aminoglycosides.
- Gastrointestinal bleeding caused by NSAIDs.
- Nephrotoxicity of ciclosporin.

Pharmacokinetic variation leading to dose-related adverse drug reactions

Variation in the hepatic metabolism of a drug is one of the major pharmacokinetic factors contributing to dose-related adverse effects. Alterations in hepatic metabolism can terminate the desired effect of a drug, generate active metabolites that are therapeutically important or generate metabolites that contribute directly to adverse effects. Renal,

cardiac and thyroid disease are also important causes of pharmacokinetic variation that predispose to adverse drug reactions (see Section 4).

Alternatively, pharmacogenetic variation can lead to adverse drug reactions. Some of the enzymes involved in the metabolic pathways of drug metabolism are subject to genetic polymorphism (see Table 7). Three examples are discussed below.

Cytochrome P450 2D6

A number of clinically important drugs are oxidised principally by one isoenzyme of cytochrome P450 (CYP), CYP 2D6 (see Table 7), a route of metabolism also known as the sparteine/debrisoquine oxidative pathway. The activity of CYP 2D6 is largely genetically determined, and the general European population segregates into two phenotypes: extensive metabolisers (90–95%) and poor metabolisers (5–10%). Poor metabolisers are homozygous for an autosomal recessive allele and extensive metabolisers are homozygous dominants or heterozygous. Poor metabolisers have no CYP 2D6 activity.

The clinical relevance of the CYP 2D6 polymorphism is most apparent for drugs that have a low therapeutic/toxic ratio. For instance, if given to a poor metaboliser:

- metoprolol may cause excessive beta blockade;

- tricyclic antidepressants have a greater risk of adverse anticholinergic effects;

- codeine cannot be converted to the active metabolite (morphine), resulting in inadequate analgesia.

Acetylator status

In the early 1950s, it was noticed that there was large variation in the metabolism of the antituberculous drug isoniazid, and distribution histograms of the percentage of isoniazid excreted unchanged in the urine of those taking it showed a bimodal distribution. Isoniazid is metabolised in the liver by a process of acetylation and this bimodal distribution suggested that individuals are either fast or slow acetylators. Like CYP 2D6, acetylator status is inherited in a simple Mendelian manner, slow acetylators being autosomal recessive homozygotes and fast acetylators heterozygotes or autosomal dominant homozygotes. There are marked differences in the relative proportions of slow and fast acetylators in different racial groups. Acetylator status is not only relevant to isoniazid; other drugs of clinical significance are inactivated by the same enzymatic process (Table 29).

The significance of acetylator status for adverse drug reactions is that slow acetylators will achieve a higher plasma concentration of a drug metabolised by this pathway for a given dose than fast acetylators. Although this may result in a greater therapeutic effect (as in the antihypertensive effect of hydralazine), it also gives rise to adverse effects at

dosages normally used in the treatment of disease. Alternatively, fast acetylators may be more at risk of an adverse drug reaction if the acetylated metabolite is also active. For example, fast acetylators may be at greater risk of isoniazid-induced hepatitis because the acetylated metabolite (acetylhydrazine) is further metabolised to a potent alkylating agent, which can covalently bind to liver cells.

Thiopurine methyltransferase

Example 23: 'Over-immunosuppression'

A 43-year-old man undergoes renal transplantation for end-stage renal disease and is immunosuppressed with appropriate doses of ciclosporin, azathioprine and prednisolone. After transplantation he develops a rapidly progressive pancytopenia.

Clinical approach

Azathioprine is a synthetic nucleotide used extensively as an immunosuppressant in organ transplantation and autoimmune disease. It is converted to the active metabolite 6-mercaptopurine, which disrupts normal purine incorporation into nucleic acids and is therefore cytotoxic. Pancytopenia caused by

marrow toxicity is a well-recognised complication of therapy with azathioprine and other thiopurines. The rapid development of severe pancytopenia at appropriate therapeutic doses of azathioprine should alert you to the possibilities of a drug interaction or a pharmacogenetic idiosyncrasy resulting in increased exposure to the cytotoxic metabolite of azathioprine. A close examination of the drug chart will reveal any co-prescribed medications that might be implicated, and the dose of azathioprine should be carefully checked.

The metabolism of azathioprine and related thiopurines (6-mercaptopurine and 6-thioguanine) is the result of the action of two enzymes: xanthine oxidase and thiopurine methyltransferase (TPMT) (Fig. 25). A deficiency in the activity of either enzyme can result in the accumulation of toxic metabolites that produce profound marrow suppression.

- Allopurinol inhibits xanthine oxidase, and significant reductions in the dose of azathioprine are required when the two drugs are co-prescribed.
- Low activity of TPMT is inherited as a rare autosomal recessive trait (1 in 300 whites; 11% prevalence of the heterozygous state), and the administration of appropriate therapeutic doses of azathioprine to such individuals results in severe marrow toxicity.

This patient was found to be a low TPMT metaboliser by polymerase chain reaction-based analysis; azathioprine was withdrawn and his marrow gradually recovered.

Could the problem have been avoided?

Pre-screening for autosomal recessive TPMT deficiency could have prevented the problem from arising. However, given the close monitoring of patients after the commencement of azathioprine therapy, the rarity of the condition and the high cost of screening, this approach is not routinely employed at present.

Drug	Drug class	Adverse reaction
Isoniazid	Antibacterial	Peripheral neuropathy
Procainamide	Antiarrhythmic	Lupus-like syndrome
Hydralazine	Vasodilator	Lupus-like syndrome
Sulfasalazine	Sulphonamide	Haemolysis
Dapsone	Sulphonamide	Haemolysis
Phenelzine	MAO inhibitor	MAO inhibitor toxicity

TABLE 29 DOSE-RELATED ADVERSE DRUG REACTIONS ARISING FROM SLOW ACETYLATOR STATUS

MAO, monoamine oxidase.

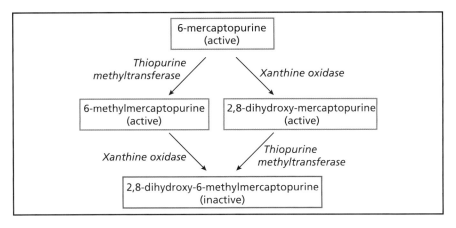

▲ **Fig. 25** The pathway for metabolism of thiopurine cytotoxic agents.

In the future, genetic profiling of patients for all pharmacogenetic variables may become a reality. If so, prescribers will need to have access to this information for all patients and be expected to use it to aid their prescribing.

Pharmacodynamic variation leading to dose-related adverse drug reactions

The pharmacodynamics of some commonly prescribed drugs may be altered by the effect of disease or by the physiological status of the patient, for example fluid and electrolyte balance. Such effects are usually dose related.

Example 24: More trouble with the foxglove

A 74-year-old woman with long-standing atrial fibrillation controlled with digoxin 250 µg/day develops mild heart failure; her doctor gives her furosemide at a dose of 40 mg/day. Six weeks later she complains of nausea, weakness and blurring of vision. Her plasma digoxin concentration is 2.8 nmol/L (2.0 ng/mL, ie at the top of the therapeutic range) and her potassium is 2.7 mmol/L. She is in complete heart block.

Clinical approach

Although the digoxin concentration taken more than 6 hours after the last dose of digoxin is not significantly elevated, the patient has symptoms of digoxin toxicity. The existence of hypokalaemia makes the diagnosis of digoxin toxicity very likely and, with correction of plasma potassium and discontinuation of digitalis, her symptoms resolved over 3 days. Her heart failure was then treated with an angiotensin-converting enzyme inhibitor as well as the loop diuretic. This combination did not result in hypokalaemia and she was able to tolerate her digoxin again at a reduced dose of 187.5 µg daily.

This is an example of a dose-related toxic effect of digoxin brought about by hypokalaemia (a pharmacodynamic rather than a pharmacokinetic interaction). Digoxin binds to, and inhibits, the Na^+/K^+-ATPase, and the affinity of this interaction is enhanced in the presence of a low extracellular potassium.

Dose-related anaphylactoid reaction

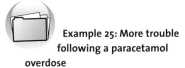

Example 25: More trouble following a paracetamol overdose

An 18-year-old unemployed man is admitted to hospital 6 hours after taking 60 tablets of paracetamol 500 mg. Blood is taken for plasma paracetamol concentration and, as he has taken a significant overdose, an infusion of *N*-acetylcysteine is started. Ten minutes after the end of the loading dose of *N*-acetylcysteine, he becomes flushed, dizzy, anxious and wheezy, and his BP falls to 85/62 mmHg.

Clinical approach

An anaphylactoid reaction is diagnosed and the *N*-acetylcysteine infusion is discontinued. He is treated with intravenous chlorpheniramine and hydrocortisone, as well as nebulised salbutamol. After 1 L of saline, his BP is restored to normal and he is well. His plasma paracetamol concentration is reported as 1.8 mmol/L. The *N*-acetylcysteine is restarted at the maintenance level and he remains asymptomatic and makes an uneventful recovery.

Although clinically indistinguishable from an anaphylactic reaction, this was a dose-related anaphylactoid reaction caused by a direct effect of *N*-acetylcysteine on mast cell and basophil degranulation. Unlike an anaphylactic reaction, there is no involvement of IgE and hence it is almost always safe to restart the infusion, albeit at a dose lower than that which precipitated the problem.

5.5 Non-dose-related adverse drug reactions (type B)

Non-dose-related adverse drug reactions (Table 30) are unrelated to the known pharmacology of the drug and are thus difficult to predict. They arise by two main mechanisms: immunological reactions and genetic variations.

TABLE 30 EXAMPLES OF NON-DOSE-RELATED ADVERSE DRUG REACTIONS

Immunological reactions	Anaphylaxis	Penicillin
	Thrombocytopenia	Quinine
	Acute interstitial nephritis	Penicillin
	Contact dermatitis	Topical local anaesthetic creams
Pseudoallergic reactions	Ampicillin rash	Patients with Epstein–Barr virus infection (glandular fever)
Genetic variation	G6PD deficiency	Haemolysis caused by oxidant drugs
	Acute intermittent porphyria	Associated with enzyme-inducing drugs, eg rifampicin
	Methaemoglobin reductase deficiency	Methaemoglobinaemia resulting from oxidant drugs
	Malignant hyperpyrexia	Suxamethonium or halothane
	Periodic paralysis	Drugs that alter plasma potassium concentrations
	Glaucoma	Glucocorticoids

G6PD, glucose-6-phosphate dehydrogenase.

Immunologically mediated adverse drug reactions

Immunologically mediated adverse drug reactions pose significant therapeutic problems. They are almost always unpredictable and often severe, so it is virtually impossible to be forewarned of the potential immunogenicity of a new drug from preclinical animal testing.

It is generally true that only molecules with a molecular mass of more than 1,000 kDa are capable of acting as immunogens, and yet most drugs are small molecules with a molecular mass of less than 500 kDa. Small molecules must therefore become covalently bound to macromolecules to be able to elicit an immune response (the hapten hypothesis of drug hypersensitivity).

Almost any drug can give rise to an allergic response, but it is clear that some drugs are particularly likely to cause hypersensitivity reactions. However, even these drugs do not provoke allergic reactions in most patients, and it is likely that genetic factors play an important role in susceptibility to drug allergy.

> ⚠ **Patients with asthma, hay fever or eczema (so-called 'atopic' individuals) and those with hereditary angio-oedema are more at risk of developing drug allergies, particularly to penicillin.**

Some drugs may conjugate to macromolecules and thus become immunogenic (eg penicillin, which undergoes spontaneous degradation in solution to chemically reactive products), whereas others may need to be converted enzymatically to reactive metabolites that then bind covalently to proteins (eg the antimalarial drug amodiaquine). The immunogenic potential of a drug is further influenced by the ability of detoxification mechanisms to clear such immunogens. Some drugs are readily converted to reactive metabolites that can bind to macromolecules, yet are rarely immunogenic (eg ethinylestradiol); this may be because the reactive metabolites or any conjugates formed are rapidly detoxified.

Immunogens may induce the formation of specific antibodies, reacting only with the parent drug compound, or they may result in the formation of antibodies that can cross-react with other antigens (eg autoantigens). As well as antibody-mediated effects, drugs can initiate antibody-independent T-cell-mediated reactions.

Do immune responses to drugs matter?

The formation of drug–macromolecule immunogens occurs commonly and, in the case of some drugs, probably in all recipients. Many individuals will produce an antibody response, but relatively few go on to develop the full allergic drug reaction and the determinants of individual sensitivity are largely unknown. Most immune responses to drugs are not associated with the development of hypersensitivity reactions and appear to be harmless or of little importance. Sometimes antibodies directed against a drug may diminish its effect, eg the thrombolytic drug streptokinase is generally given in large doses because many individuals have antibodies that react with streptokinase and effectively neutralise a substantial proportion of the dose administered.

Drug hypersensitivity reactions have been classified on the basis of immunological mechanisms as shown in Table 31. Although some drugs are associated with particular types of hypersensitivity reactions, a few (eg penicillin) may be involved with more than one type of reaction (Table 32). Furthermore, the precise clinical manifestations of drug hypersensitivity reactions can vary considerably, and hence strict adherence to immunological classifications is not particularly helpful in clinical practice. Hypersensitivity reactions may manifest as fever, rash, a lupus-like

TABLE 31 THE GELL AND COOMBS CLASSIFICATION OF HYPERSENSITIVITY

Classification	Mechanism	Example
Type I: immediate hypersensitivity	IgE fixed to mast cells/basophils binds multivalent drug–hapten antigens free in circulation. Degranulation of mast cells results in release of vasoactive and inflammatory mediators such as histamine. Typically develops within minutes and lasts 1–2 hours	Anaphylaxis to radio-opaque iodine-containing contrast media
Type II: cytotoxic	Antigen consists of drug combined with a protein embedded in a cell membrane. Binding and cross-linking of IgG, IgM or IgA free in circulation results in complement fixation and cell lysis	Rifampicin-induced thrombocytopenia and haemolytic anaemia
Type III: immune complex	Drug acts as a free antigen in excess in the circulation and forms immune complexes with IgG, which are deposited in postcapillary venules, thus causing tissue damage. Can develop 1–3 weeks after exposure	NSAID-related glomerulonephritis
Type IV: cell mediated	T-killer cell interacts with drug–hapten antigen on cell membrane leading directly to cell death	Contact dermatitis

TABLE 32 HYPERSENSITIVITY REACTIONS ASSOCIATED WITH PENICILLIN

Clinical presentation	Immunological classification
Acute anaphylaxis: urticaria, angio-oedema, hypotension and bronchospasm	Type I
Haemolytic anaemia, seen usually with high dosages and prolonged treatment	Type II
Fever, urticaria, maculopapular rash, arthritis and glomerulonephritis (serum sickness)	Type III
Contact dermatitis from skin creams containing penicillin	Type IV

syndrome, blood dyscrasias, and hepatic and respiratory disorders.

The following are examples that illustrate some of the clinical presentations of immunologically mediated adverse drug reactions and demonstrate possible mechanisms underlying drug hypersensitivity.

Anaphylactic reactions

Example 26: Twice bitten

A 24-year-old man is bitten by a dog and attends the Emergency Department where he is given co-amoxiclav. One hour after taking the first dose at home, he becomes very unwell with severe itching, wheezing and chest tightness. His GP is called and diagnoses an acute anaphylactic reaction and, in view of the patient's

worsening condition, administers intramuscular epinephrine, intravenous hydrocortisone and chlorpheniramine, and nebulised salbutamol. The patient is admitted to hospital and makes a full and rapid recovery. On further questioning, he recalls a previous less severe reaction to penicillin given for recurrent tonsillitis as a child.

Clinical approach

Anaphylactic or type I immediate hypersensitivity reactions occur in about 1–5 in 10,000 people treated with penicillins. The reaction is caused by an antigen (the penicillin) reacting with IgE antibodies on the surface of mast cells and basophils. This results in the release of a wide range of vasoactive and inflammatory mediators including histamine, serotonin (5-hydroxytryptamine) and leukotrienes. In the case of allergic reactions to penicillin, there is cross-reaction with cephalosporins in about 10% of cases.

To minimise the risk of acute anaphylactic reactions, it is essential to take a full drug and allergy history from all patients. The difficulty lies in knowing how to interpret reports of rashes associated with penicillin usage, but the safest thing to do is to avoid penicillins if there is doubt.

Immune-mediated hepatitis

The inhalational anaesthetic agent halothane causes a mild and transient derangement of hepatocellular function in up to 30% of patients. Serum transaminases are increased and liver histology may show mild focal necrotic lesions. Previous exposure to halothane is not a prerequisite for this reaction, which is caused by

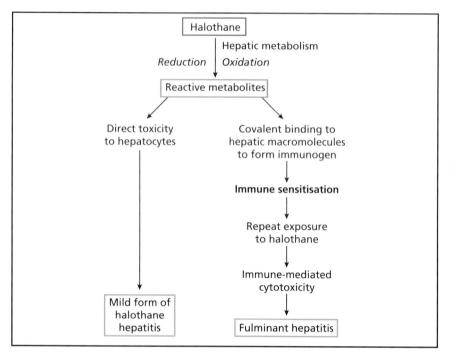

Fig. 26 The steps involved in halothane-induced liver damage

hepatic macromolecules and become antigenic. When this occurs immune-mediated cytotoxicity may result in progression to fulminant hepatitis if the patient has a further general anaesthetic containing halothane.

Halothane hepatitis

As might be anticipated in a hypersensitivity reaction, the incidence of fulminant hepatitis increases after multiple exposures to halothane, and so repeated use within 3 months should be avoided. It is also advisable to avoid the use of halothane in any patient with previously unexplained postoperative jaundice.

Immune haemolytic anaemias

Drugs can give rise to haemolysis by direct chemical means (eg the action of oxidant drugs in G6PD deficiency) or via immune-mediated red cell destruction. For immune haemolysis to occur, antibodies or complement must be bound to the red cell, and this can arise by three main mechanisms (Table 33).

reactive metabolic intermediates of halothane binding directly to hepatocytes. Much more rarely (about 1 in 35,000 patients), a severe and fulminant hepatitis occurs (with a mortality rate of about 90%) and this is the result of an immunologically mediated reaction (Fig. 26).

In the liver, halothane is metabolised by reduction and oxidation. The reduced metabolites react directly with hepatocytes and are responsible for the mild hepatic disturbance. Halothane is oxidised by a hepatic cytochrome P450 enzyme to trifluoroacetyl chloride, which can covalently bind to

Drugs	Mechanism of haemolysis	Antibody	Comment
Penicillin Cephalosporins	Covalent binding of drug to red cell membranes	IgG	When penicillin is used in high doses for a prolonged period of time, the drug binds covalently to red cell membranes and this hapten–membrane complex may then elicit an immune response, with the production of specific, mainly IgG, antibodies. Antigen–antibody cross-linking occurs and extravascular haemolysis results. When the drug is discontinued, the haemolysis resolves but may recur on second exposure. These antibodies can cross-react with cephalosporins and cause similar effects
Quinine Quinidine Sulphonamides Isoniazid Rifampicin	Immune complex association with red cell membranes and subsequent fixation of complement	IgM	Covalent binding of drugs or their metabolites to circulating free proteins is thought to stimulate antibody production, mainly of the IgM type. In the presence of the drug, antigen–antibody complexes form and then associate with red cell membranes, complement is activated and profound intravascular haemolysis occurs. Haemolysis does not occur with the first dose of drug but on second or subsequent exposure, and it resolves promptly on withdrawal of the drug
Methyldopa Levodopa Mefenamic acid	Autoantibodies that recognise red cell components	IgG	When given over a long period of time these drugs can give rise to the formation of IgG antibodies, which cross-react with components in the red cell membrane and cause extravascular haemolysis. This is rarely severe and ceases when the drug is withdrawn

TABLE 33 DRUGS THAT MOST COMMONLY CAUSE IMMUNE HAEMOLYTIC ANAEMIA

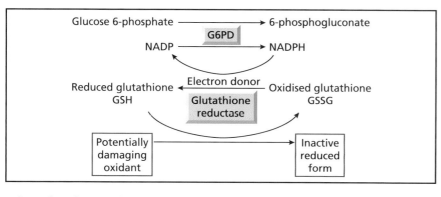

▲ **Fig. 27** The pathways involved in the generation of reduced glutathione in red cells.

TABLE 34 OXIDANT DRUGS THAT CAN PRECIPITATE HAEMOLYSIS IN PATIENTS WITH G6PD DEFICIENCY

Drug class	Common examples
Analgesics	Aspirin
Antibiotics	Chloramphenicol
	Nitrofurantoin
	Sulphonamides
Antimalarials	Primaquine
	Dapsone
	Quinine
Miscellaneous	Quinidine and vitamin K

Genetic variation and susceptibility to non-dose-related adverse drug reactions

Glucose-6-phosphate dehydrogenase deficiency

> G6PD deficiency is the most common human enzymopathy, affecting over 10 million people worldwide. Several hundred biochemically or genetically different forms of the enzyme have been identified, but in essence the condition arises from reduced enzymatic activity of G6PD, which in severe cases results in red cells being more susceptible to damage from oxidising agents.

G6PD is an enzyme that reduces nicotinamide adenine dinucleotide phosphate (NADP) to NADPH (see *Biochemistry and Metabolism*, Carbohydrates). NADPH is required to convert oxidised glutathione to the reduced form, and it is this reduced glutathione that protects erythrocytes from damage by oxidising agents (Fig. 27). Certain drugs act as oxidants and may precipitate haemolysis in patients who are deficient in G6PD (Table 34). The most severe effects of G6PD deficiency are seen in individuals in whom enzyme activity is below 5% of normal. Less severe forms, in which enzyme activity is between 10 and 30% of normal, usually become apparent only when affected individuals are treated with those drugs that have the greatest potential as oxidising agents.

Acute porphyria

> The acute porphyrias are a group of genetically determined metabolic disorders characterised by defects in the enzymes associated with porphyrin and haem biosynthesis. In all the various types, there is increased activity of the rate-limiting enzyme δ-aminolaevulinic acid (ALA) synthase; the different forms are characterised by specific enzyme defects further along the pathway of porphyrin synthesis (Fig. 28). (See *Biochemistry and Metabolism*, Haem.)

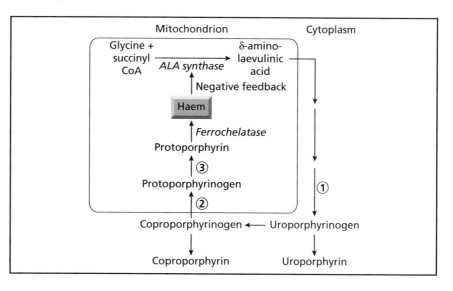

▲ **Fig. 28** The pathways involved in porphyrin and haem biosynthesis: (**1**) the enzymatic step involving uroporphyrinogen I synthase and uroporphyrinogen cosynthetase, which is affected in acute intermittent porphyria; (**2**) the reaction involving coproporphyrinogen oxidase, which is deficient in hereditary coproporphyria; (**3**) the reaction catalysed by protoporphyrinogen oxidase, which is deficient in variegate porphyria.

TABLE 35 SOME OF THE MORE COMMONLY PRESCRIBED DRUGS WHICH HAVE BEEN REPORTED TO PRECIPITATE AN ATTACK OF ACUTE PORPHYRIA

Drug class	Common examples
Antibiotics	Sulphonamides, tetracycline, isoniazid, griseofulvin, nitrofurantoin, rifampicin
Anticonvulsants	Phenytoin, carbamazepine, ethosuximide, primidone
Oral hypoglycaemic agents	Tolbutamide, chlorpropamide
Sedatives/hypnotics	Chlordiazepoxide, nitrazepam, oxazepam, barbiturates
Sex steroids	Oral contraceptives, oestrogens
Miscellaneous	Ethanol, imipramine, methyldopa

Acute intermittent porphyria, hereditary coproporphyria and variegate porphyria can all present acutely with abdominal and neuropsychiatric symptoms. In hereditary coproporphyria and variegate porphyria, there may also be skin photosensitivity. Patients with a genetic predisposition to acute porphyria may develop an acute attack after exposure to alcohol or certain drugs, which in general are inducers of hepatic monooxygenase enzymes (Table 35).

The way in which the accumulation of porphyrins causes symptoms is not clear. Porphyrins are known to be photosensitising agents and the cutaneous manifestations of the porphyrias may be the result of damage from photochemical reactions arising as a result of the absorption by porphyrins of radiant energy in the ultraviolet region of the spectrum. The abdominal and neuropsychiatric manifestations of the disease are not so readily explained.

FURTHER READING

Chapel H, Haeney M, Misbah S, *et al. Essential Clinical Immunology*, 5th edn. Oxford: Blackwell Science, 2006.

Journal of Hepatology 1997; 26 (Suppl. 2) is devoted to drugs and the liver.

Pirmohamed M, Madden S and Park BK. Idiosyncratic drug reactions: metabolic bioactivation as a pathogenic mechanism. *Clin. Pharmacokinet.* 1996; 31: 215–30.

5.6 Adverse reactions caused by long-term effects of drugs (type C)

There may be problems of cumulative toxicity when drugs are taken over a long period of time. Recognising this sort of gradual drug toxicity is more difficult than many of the reactions described so far because the index of suspicion for adverse drug reactions is often low when the drug concerned has been taken for a long time. The most common example is the prolonged use of corticosteroids giving rise to cushingoid features and hypothalamic–pituitary–adrenal axis suppression. Other examples include prolonged use of amiodarone, lithium and chloroquine.

Amiodarone

 Example 27: It seemed useful at the time

A 59-year-old man with troublesome paroxysmal atrial fibrillation and normal left ventricular function is treated with amiodarone resulting in useful suppression of symptoms. Three years later he re-presents with progressive breathlessness and his GP finds that he has widespread fine crepitations in both lung fields. A CXR and CT scan show that he has diffuse interstitial infiltrates, and a CT cut through the liver demonstrates high signal intensity (Fig. 29). The diagnosis of amiodarone lung was made, the drug was discontinued and he was treated with high-dose steroids.

Clinical approach

The antiarrhythmic drug amiodarone is very lipophilic and highly tissue bound, with an elimination half-life of about 45–60 days. Gradual tissue accumulation of amiodarone and its principal metabolite desethylamiodarone is associated with the deposition of lipofuscin in the organs in which long-term toxic effects are most commonly seen. However, the relationship between lipofuscin deposition and the adverse effects of amiodarone is not absolute, because many patients will accumulate lipofuscin but not have evidence of adverse effects.

Lithium

Lithium is widely used in the long-term treatment of bipolar affective disorder, but about 5% of patients develop benign diffuse enlargement of the thyroid gland. Lithium interferes with the iodination of tyrosine, and as a result thyroxine output from the thyroid falls. Most patients taking lithium long term are euthyroid, because there is a compensatory rise in thyroid-stimulating hormone (TSH) release

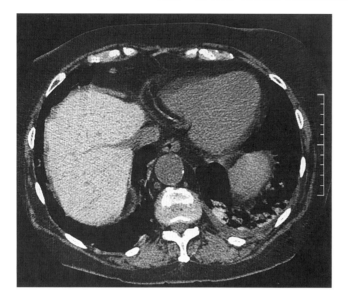

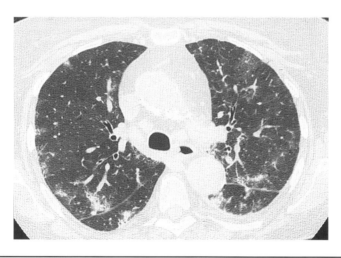

▲ **Fig. 29** (**a**) CT scan of the liver. The liver is hyperdense [118 Hounsfield units (HU)] and the consolidation in the left lower lobe is also hyperdense (131 HU). Both of these characteristics are typical of iodine deposition and the combination is pathognomonic of amiodarone accumulation. (**b**) High-resolution CT scan of the lung: bilateral peripheral ground-glass change with interstitial fibrosis. (By kind permission of Dr N. Moore.)

from the pituitary. It is this rise in TSH that causes the diffuse enlargement of the thyroid gland which, if troublesome, can be treated with thyroxine, which suppresses TSH production.

Chloroquine

The antimalarial drug chloroquine can cause a lichenoid skin eruption when used long term, but is otherwise quite well tolerated in the dosages used for the prophylaxis of malaria. Chloroquine also has a

place in the treatment of autoimmune rheumatic diseases, such as rheumatoid arthritis and lupus erythematosus, when it may be used in substantially higher doses than in malaria prophylaxis. Under these circumstances irreversible retinopathy is a serious adverse effect and is related to the high affinity of chloroquine for melanin, which results in its accumulation in retinal pigment. Regular ophthalmological examination to detect early subclinical changes in

retinal function is essential to avoid progressive visual loss in patients on high-dose chloroquine.

5.7 Adverse reactions caused by delayed effects of drugs (type D)

⚠ 'Some drugs have been appropriately called "wonder drugs" inasmuch as one wonders what they will do next.' (Samuel E. Stumpf)

Carcinogenesis

When adverse reactions occur months or years after a drug has been discontinued, it is extremely difficult to identify a causal relationship. Drug-induced neoplasia is a particular concern because it is often not apparent for many years after the introduction of a drug, and it may not have been anticipated in preclinical toxicological testing in animals.

A high proportion of patients receiving immunosuppressive therapy after organ transplantation develop malignant lymphomas (up to 20% in some series). It seems likely that this is a result of the depression of the protective immune response rather than any direct carcinogenic effect of immunosuppressive drugs. However, the risks of lymphoma in this group of patients are usually more than balanced by the severity of the illness for which transplantation was initially performed.

In the early 1970s, there were several reports of a very rare tumour (vaginal adenocarcinoma) in young girls whose mothers had been given oestrogens (diethylstilbestrol) during the first trimester of pregnancy for the treatment of uterine bleeding. The spontaneous incidence of this tumour in girls whose mothers are not given diethylstilbestrol is so low that it was relatively easy to make a direct association with the drug in new cases.

Chronic overuse of analgesic drugs, particularly those containing phenacetin, causes renal papillary necrosis and ultimately renal failure. In addition, there is an association between long-term phenacetin abuse and transitional cell carcinomas of the renal tract. Although phenacetin is no longer marketed, transitional cell tumours still arise as a late complication of its use.

Teratogenic effects

The increased incidence of phocomelia (hypoplastic or aplastic limb deformities) in children born to mothers who had taken thalidomide in the first trimester of pregancy, and the subsequent withdrawal of the drug in 1961, led directly to the formation of the committee that

became the current Committee on the Safety of Medicines. Fortunately, such tragedies are rare, but many drugs have the potential to damage the fetus during pregnancy and reliable data on the teratogenic risks of drugs in humans is limited.

> Always consult the data sheet and the *British National Formulary* for any drug that you intend to use in a woman of childbearing age. If in doubt, do not prescribe.

5.8 Withdrawal reactions (type E)

Long-term treatment with some drugs causes adaptive changes in homeostatic mechanisms or induces a state of drug dependence, so that when the drug is abruptly discontinued a withdrawal reaction occurs. Perhaps the most commonly encountered withdrawal syndrome is that of delirium tremens. Benzodiazepines, opioid analgesics

and barbiturates are all associated with specific syndromes, which may arise on sudden discontinuation of therapy (or abuse).

Example 28: Don't stop taking the pills

A 73-year-old man developed nausea, vomiting and diarrhoea. His GP diagnosed food poisoning and advised that he went to bed and took plenty of fluids. Three days later he was worse and was admitted to hospital, where he was found to be severely dehydrated, hypotensive and in acute renal failure. It transpired that because of the vomiting he had felt unable to take his usual tablets, which included prednisolone 10 mg a day, prescribed for temporal arteritis 18 months earlier.

Clinical approach

This patient became dehydrated because of his diarrhoea and vomiting, but the problem was compounded by abrupt steroid withdrawal leading to an addisonian crisis. He made a good recovery with fluid and steroid replacement, and was given advice about what to do in the future if he became unwell.

TABLE 36 PRESENTATION AND MANAGEMENT OF ECSTASY (MDMA) AND COCAINE OVERDOSE			
Drug	**Mechanism of action**	**Presentation**	**Specific management**
Cocaine	Central nervous system stimulant; inhibits dopamine uptake leading to increased dopaminergic transmission and euphoria	Agitation, hyperthermia, tachycardia, hypertension and tachypnoea Chest pain and arrhythmia: acute coronary spasm Dilated pupils, restlessness, irritability, confusion, paranoid psychosis, seizures and stroke Hypersensitivity reactions	Supportive measures, active cooling, diazepam for seizures and hypertension, calcium channel antagonists and/or GTN for coronary spasm Avoid thrombolysis and beta-blockers
Ecstasy (MDMA)	An amphetamine that causes catecholamine release from presynaptic neurons Also causes massive release of serotonin Has unpredictable toxicity	Hyperthermia, hypertension and 'heat stroke' Serotonergic syndrome: flushed, tachycardic, hyperreflexic, clonus, muscular rigidity and autonomic instability Syndrome of inappropriate antidiuretic hormone secretion/excretion, cerebral oedema and seizures	Supportive measures, active cooling, diazepam and GTN for hypertension Consider specific 5HT antagonists

GTN, glyceryl trinitrate; 5HT, 5-hydroxytryptamine.

⚠ Long-term corticosteroid therapy is associated with suppression of the hypothalamic–pituitary–adrenal axis. If steroid therapy is withdrawn, adrenal insufficiency may occur either acutely or at a later stage when heightened physical stress occurs (eg infection or major surgery).

5.9 Drugs in overdose and use of illicit drugs

Deliberate self-harm often involves poisoning and overdose with medicines and/or illicit drugs. Although not strictly 'adverse effects', drugs in overdose will produce toxic and collateral effects that must be managed appropriately. Once recognised, initial management will include general supportive measures and assessment of severity and risk. Specific treatment measures may be indicated for specific poisonings. Refer to *Acute Medicine* for details of the general approach to overdose and treatment of paracetamol, salicylate, tricyclic opiate and alcohol poisoning, and to Table 36 for information related to cocaine and Ecstasy (3,4-methylenedioxymethamphetamine, MDMA) overdose.

🔑 • Always consult TOXBASE, the online clinical toxicology database, for information regarding specific management. Available at http://www.spib.axl.co.uk/
• The National Poisons Information Service (NPIS) also offers a 24-hour telephone information line. For contact details see their website at http://www.npis.org/

The processes of development of drugs from identification of molecules to their release as medicines into the marketplace are outlined in this section (Fig. 30).

6.1 Drug development

The pharmaceutical industry has been responsible for the production of many life-saving therapies that are an established part of everyday medicine. Streptokinase for the treatment of myocardial infarction, antiretroviral agents for the treatment of HIV and monoclonal antibodies against tumour necrosis factor-α for rheumatoid arthritis are all examples. However, the cost of developing new medicines is high and the primary duty of a pharmaceutical company is to return a profit for its shareholders. To offset this risk, recover the cost of the manufacture, distribution and marketing of a drug, and to return a profit, the company will lodge a patent for any new agent it develops, which will grant it the exclusive right to manufacture and sell the agent for a period of between 10 and 20 years.

The societal demand for better healthcare has increased pressures on drug development. In 2003, 650 million prescriptions were written, representing an increase of 40% over 10 years. The annual National Health Service drug budget is currently £8 billion, but increasing at a rate of 9.7% per annum.

> As individual doctors, it is our primary concern to evaluate the benefit that any new therapy might provide for our patients, and to ensure this is achieved with an acceptably low rate of harm. However, because new drugs are developed within the context of corporate profit and market forces, doctors need to be equipped with the tools to distinguish hard evidence on the efficacy of new drugs from marketing spin. The only effective way to formulate an independent and informed opinion is to understand the process of drug development and licensing, and to be able to make sense of the results of clinical trials evaluating new medicines.

Identifying molecules for development as drugs

Identification of new molecular entities follows principles outlined by Paul Ehrlich in 1915, who proposed that agents cannot act unless they are bound (to a target). Although the approach to identifying new drugs has advanced to include high-throughput screening of millions of compounds developed by medicinal chemists as well as therapies designed on the basis of molecular biological methods (and the two together, so-called combinatorial methods), the principle of identifying a 'therapeutic target' – Ehrlich's

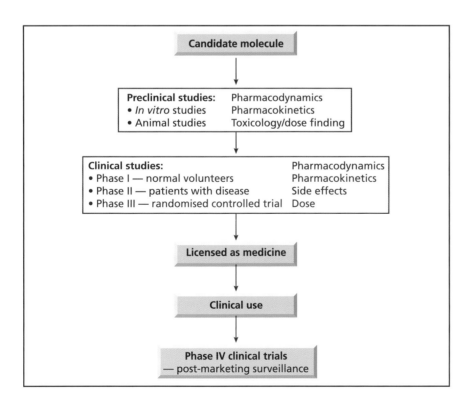

▲ **Fig. 30** Drug development: from molecule to marketplace.

receptor – remains unchanged. As an example, let us consider the identification of a new treatment for diabetes.

Insulin resistance is a common feature of type 2 diabetes and obesity. In the early 1980s, new compounds were sought that could treat these conditions by decreasing insulin resistance. Ciglitazone was selected as a promising candidate because it was shown to reduce insulin resistance in animal models of diabetes. Based on this discovery, a range of related chemical compounds, the thiazolidinediones or glitazones, was synthesised and tested for antihyperglycaemic activity in diabetic animal models. The more potent of these compounds were selected for development for use in the clinical setting.

> A number of different approaches are used to identify molecules that may have therapeutic use (Fig. 31):
>
> - screening of molecules for therapeutic effect;
> - modification of identified molecules;
> - design of molecules for a specific therapeutic purpose.

Preclinical studies of new drugs

Preclinical studies are performed either *in vitro*, eg in cell culture systems or tissues, or in animals, before giving the drug to humans. The purpose of preclinical studies is to establish the following:

- what actions the drug has (pharmacodynamics);

- how the drug is absorbed, distributed, metabolised and eliminated (pharmacokinetics);

- what toxic effects the drug has after a single dose, repeated doses and long-term administration (toxicology);

- what doses of the drug are effective but also likely to be safe.

Pharmacodynamics

Continuing with the example of the glitazones, early studies showed that these compounds suppressed insulin resistance and hyperglycaemia in genetically obese diabetic rats. Subsequent *in vitro* and animal studies revealed that they bind and activate a nuclear receptor, the peroxisome proliferator-activated receptor γ. Activation of this receptor results in the modulation of transcription of a number of insulin-responsive genes involved in the control of glucose and lipid metabolism.

Pharmacokinetics

In vitro studies of the effect of mice hepatic cytosol and microsome preparations on the glitazones predicted that these drugs would be metabolised by liver enzymes. The interaction between cytochrome P450 (CYP) enzymes and individual glitazones was also assessed *in vitro*, predicting that troglitazone and its metabolites would inhibit CYP 2C8, 2C9, 2C19 and 3A4 activity, whereas rosiglitazone and pioglitazone would be metabolised by these enzymes but would not inhibit them.

In vivo studies of glitazone pharmacokinetics in dogs and rats were used to establish that the drugs were absorbed across the gastrointestinal tract, widely distributed in tissues, metabolised in the liver and largely excreted in the bile and faeces, with the remainder being eliminated in the urine.

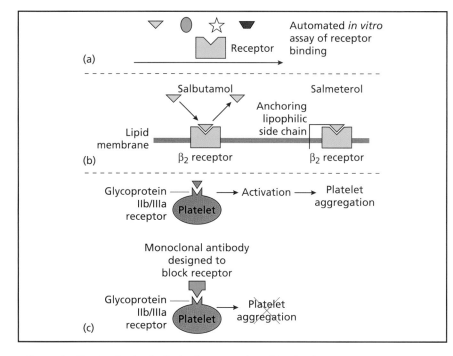

▲ **Fig. 31** Identification of molecules for development as drugs. (a) Molecules may be screened for therapeutic effect, eg by automated *in vitro* assays of binding to a specific receptor or by examination of the effect of molecules in animal models of disease. (b) Molecules may be modified from other molecules of known effect, eg salbutamol is a short-acting β₂-adrenoceptor agonist and salmeterol is a long-acting β₂-adrenoceptor agonist, because the addition of a lipophilic side chain enables it to remain anchored in the cell membrane adjacent to the β₂ adrenoceptor and slows washout from the receptor. (c) Molecules may be synthesised for a specific therapeutic purpose. Antibodies can be designed to target undesirable proteins or cells in the body, eg monoclonal antibodies that bind to the platelet glycoprotein IIb/IIIa receptor inhibit platelet aggregation.

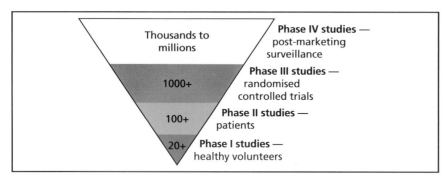

▲ **Fig. 32** Numbers of humans exposed to new drugs at different phases of development.

Toxicology

As the glitazones were likely to be given to patients over a prolonged period, long-term studies looking for carcinogenic effects of glitazones in animals were performed. Over a 2-year study some rats taking troglitazone developed haemangiosarcomas, and the tumour-inducing effects of the glitazones were also found in mouse models of familial adenomatous polyposis and sporadic colon cancer.

Limitations of preclinical studies

Preclinical studies are meant to predict what will happen when the drug is given to humans. These predictions are often difficult because drug effects, metabolism and side effects may differ between conditions *in vitro* and those *in vivo*, and between animals and humans. Preclinical studies to detect rare or long-term side effects are difficult and expensive to do.

Clinical trials: from drug to medicine

A drug is any substance that alters physiological processes in the body. A drug can be considered to be a medicine when it is licensed, and is used, to improve or maintain health. Only a small proportion of drugs that are tested for development become licensed medicines; the lengthy path that they have to follow is shown in Figs 30–32.

Phases of clinical trials

The phases that comprise clinical trials are illustrated in Fig. 32.

Phase I trials These test drug handling by healthy volunteers. They are the first tests done in humans and include the following.

- Pharmacodynamic studies: some assessment of drug actions in people without disease.

- Assessment of types and risk of side effects.

- Pharmacokinetic studies: absorption, distribution, metabolism and elimination of the drug. Potential drug interactions may also be identified at this stage.

- Dose-finding studies: determination of plasma concentration, effects and side effects at different doses to establish safety and efficacy.

Drugs that are potentially harmful, eg chemotherapeutic agents, will not be given to normal volunteers.

Phase II trials These test drug handling and effects in people with disease. They are the first tests done in patients and include the following.

- Pharmacodynamic studies: first assessment of drug efficacy in people with disease.

- Reassessment of types and risk of side effects in patients.

- Reassessment of pharmacokinetics and drug dose in patients.

Phase III trials These formally assess the effectiveness and safety (and acceptability) of the drug in people with disease. The gold-standard phase III study is the double-blind, randomised controlled trial (RCT). In the simplest form of RCT, people with the condition expected to respond to a new drug are allocated randomly into two groups: one group receives the active drug and the other placebo; drug and placebo look identical and neither the investigator nor the trial subjects know who is taking what. Both groups of subjects are monitored for treatment effects and adverse reactions, and statistical methods are used to determine whether beneficial and harmful effects are significantly different in people taking the drug from those seen in people taking placebo. RCTs can also be used to compare the safety and efficacy of a new drug with existing treatment. More details on the approach to interpreting evidence from clinical trials are given in the *Statistics, Epidemiology, Clinical Trials and Meta-Analyses* section of this module.

Licensing

For a drug to be used in the UK it needs to have a product licence. To reach this stage, the manufacturer is required to present evidence from preclinical and clinical trials demonstrating that the drug has an effect on the condition it is indicated for, that the material is of the required quality and purity having being manufactured to a high standard and safety, and that it is safe with no serious adverse reactions.

The condition of safety is difficult to establish absolutely at the time at which the licence may be awarded, because by this stage the new drug may only have been tested on a few thousand individuals for a relatively short time. For this reason, newly licensed drugs are exposed to a period of continued monitoring after they are released into the market, termed post-marketing surveillance. It is also important to note that, in most instances, a licence is granted without the requirement for a direct comparative evaluation against the best existing standard treatment.

A product licence gives reassurance about efficacy, safety and pharmaceutical quality. Safety data at the time of product launch are always very limited and the true safety may take years to become apparent (see Fig. 30). Evidence of efficacy does not necessarily mean that a drug is an effective treatment, or better than existing therapies for the same condition.

Licensing process This can follow one of three routes (Fig. 33).

- The first is through the executive arm of the UK Licensing Authority, the Medicines and Healthcare products Regulatory Agency (MHRA), a division of the Department of Health, which is unique amongst agencies of its kind in that it is almost entirely funded by fees gained from services provided to the pharmaceutical industry. Approval by the MHRA will mean a medication can be used in the UK. The Commission of Human Medicines (CHM) is an independent advisory body also set up under the same Act of Parliament as the MHRA, and its function is to advise the MHRA on drug approvals.

- The second route is through the centralised approval system of the European Medicines Evaluation Agency (EMEA). Within the EMEA, applications are processed by the Committee for Proprietary Medicinal Products (CPMP), whose licence has jurisdiction in all member states of the European Community. The CPMP may contract out assessments to member states, through agencies such as the MHRA, and will then hear the completed assessment and make a licensing decision.

- The third route to licensing is through a process known as 'mutual recognition'. Under this scheme a pharmaceutical company will apply for a licence in one European country and, once granted, it may then seek approval for use in other member states on this basis. Objections and appeals within the mutual recognition process are overseen by the CPMP within the EMEA.

Marketing authorisations are given in the first instance for a period of 5 years, after which they can be either renewed for a limited period (when additional safety and efficacy data are reviewed) or for an unlimited period.

Preparation for regulatory application is time-consuming. By the time a drug is licensed there may only be about 10 years remaining on the valuable patent that provides for market exclusivity. It is during these 10 years or so that the company needs to recoup its investment in the development of the drug. Regulatory processes reduce patent life, which led to the introduction of the Supplementary Protection Certificate in 1993 in the UK and in some other EU states, which allows for an additional 5 years of exclusivity if granted.

Post-marketing surveillance (phase IV clinical trials)

News report, 1 December 1997: troglitazone withdrawn in UK because of serious hepatic reactions

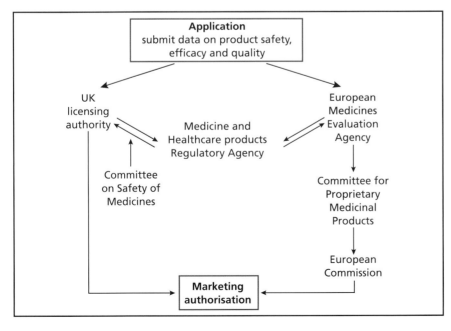

▲ **Fig. 33** Licensing mechanisms for new drugs.

Application
submit data on product safety, efficacy and quality

UK licensing authority

Medicine and Healthcare products Regulatory Agency

European Medicines Evaluation Agency

Committee on Safety of Medicines

Committee for Proprietary Medicinal Products

European Commission

Marketing authorisation

Approximately 370,000 patients worldwide have been treated with troglitazone for at least 3 months and 130 cases (6 fatal) of hepatic reactions to the drug have been reported. These included severe hepatocellular damage, hepatic necrosis and hepatic failure. At present these reactions are unpredictable; no clear patient risk factors for the development of hepatic reactions have been identified, and the reactions can occur from 2 weeks to 8 months after starting the drug. Overall it is considered that, based on present information, the risks of troglitazone therapy outweigh the potential benefits. It has therefore been voluntarily withdrawn from the UK as from 1 December 1997 by the companies concerned, who have informed doctors and pharmacists by letter. Any patient who is taking troglitazone should be transferred to an alternative therapy for the treatment of their diabetes.

By the time a medicine gets to market it may have been tested in a few thousand people, including perhaps around 1,000 people in an RCT (see Fig. 32). These recipients will have been carefully chosen; people at high risk of side effects, such as the very young or old or those with hepatic or renal impairment, will probably have been excluded from the phase III studies. Adverse effects of a drug may not have been identified if they:

- are uncommon;

- occur in a vulnerable group of people not included in the clinical trial;

- result from unexpected reactions with other drugs, not predicted from trials.

It is important that adverse reactions are detected and acted upon, even after a licence has been granted. Pharmacovigilance is the process of monitoring the use of medicines in everyday practice to detect previously unrecognised adverse reactions (Fig. 34). Pharmacovigilance in the UK is the responsibility of the MHRA, with the assistance of the CHM. The MHRA also functions to ensure good clinical practice in ongoing clinical trials, and will intermittently inspect pre- and post-licensing studies for this purpose.

Adverse reactions to marketed drugs are detected by the following.

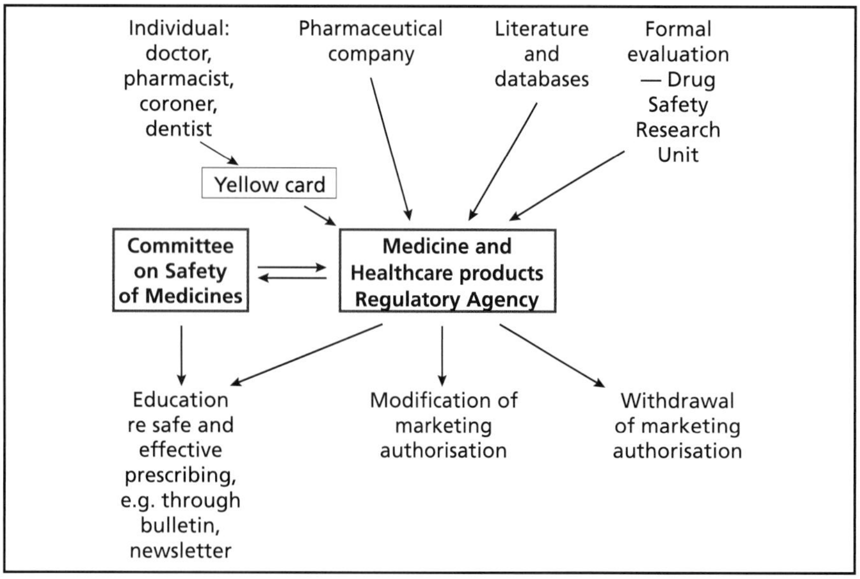

- Voluntary reporting: in clinical practice, if an adverse drug reaction is suspected, the professional (doctor, dentist, pharmacist or coroner) voluntarily reports this to the CHM using the Yellow Card Scheme (see 'Key point' below).

- Compulsory reporting: pharmaceutical companies are under a statutory obligation to report any suspected adverse reactions that come to their attention, eg during unpublished clinical trials.

- Literature and database surveillance: reports of adverse reactions in the world literature and from morbidity and mortality databases are documented.

- Formal study: the Drug Safety Research Unit in Southampton carries out formal assessment of selected medicines. The Prescription Pricing Authority is asked to identify all prescriptions of the chosen medicine during a set time period. At the end of this period, questionnaires are sent to the doctors who have written each prescription, asking whether the patient experienced any adverse reaction on the drug. These data give an estimate of the types and frequency of adverse reactions caused by that medicine.

Adverse reactions may be identified and found to be more frequent than expected or shown to affect particular patient subgroups during post-marketing surveillance. These findings may lead to the following.

- Changes in marketing authorisation, eg restrictions in use or refinement of dose instructions, which enable medicines to be used more safely and effectively.

▲**Fig. 34** Pharmacovigilance.

- Withdrawal of medicines from the market if they are associated with an unacceptable hazard.

- Education of healthcare professionals about safer and more effective use of products through modification of product information, newsletters and bulletins.

Practical guide to reporting an adverse drug reaction

What should I report?

An adverse drug reaction (ADR) is a harmful and unintended effect of a medicine during its use in prevention, treatment or diagnosis of disease. You should report definite or suspected drug reactions (even if not proven) if:

- a product has received its licence or its use has changed in the last 2 years (marked ▼ in the *British National Formulary*).
- the adverse reaction to ANY product is severe, ie 'is fatal, life threatening, disabling, incapacitating, or which results in or prolongs hospitalisation and/or is medically significant'. *If in doubt, report.*

How do I report an ADR?

You fill in a yellow card, which can be found at the back of the *British National Formulary*. The information required for the report is clearly requested on the card. Even if some of this information is not available, the card should still be sent in. Pharmacists are usually a good source of yellow cards, advice or help if you have problems with this system.

What happens next?

After reporting a suspected ADR, you will receive an acknowledgement letter and a copy of the report to be added to the patient's notes. Cases are then entered on the Adverse Drug Reactions On-Line Information Tracking (ADROIT) database of the MHRA. Your information helps the MHRA to monitor product safety and take action to minimise the risks and maximise the benefits of medicines.

FURTHER READING

Medicines and Healthcare products Regulatory Agency: http://www.mhra.gov.uk/

6.2 Rational prescribing

Entry of new drugs into the market

A medicine receives a licence (marketing authorisation) when it has been judged as safe, effective and of sufficient quality by the licensing authority (Fig. 35). A licence, however, does not imply that the drug is better than other drugs also available for the same condition. Once a drug reaches the market, its place in therapy therefore needs to be determined. Ideally, this should be done using critical appraisal of the available evidence.

Drugs should be assessed in comparison with other drugs already available for treatment of the same condition on the basis of the following.

- Efficacy: does the new drug work better than existing treatments available for the same condition?

- Safety: does the new drug have fewer, or more acceptable, side effects than existing treatments?

- Acceptability: is it easier for patients to take this new drug?

- Cost: where a new drug does not represent a clinically significant advantage in terms of efficacy, safety or acceptability, it may still be adopted for use if it is as good as, and cheaper than, existing medicines.

If the new drug meets one of these criteria, and particularly if it makes a clinically significant improvement to current therapy, then it is likely to be adopted for use.

Clinical versus statistical significance

Improvements in treatment with a new drug can be statistically significant without being clinically significant, eg a drug for the treatment of dementia may cause a statistical improvement in a dementia score compared with placebo. However, if the magnitude of that improvement is small and does not correspond to an improvement in activities of daily living, the improvement may not be considered to be clinically significant or worth the effort and expense of therapy.

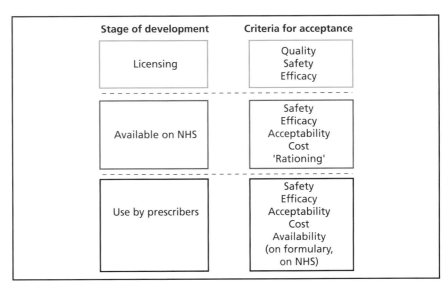

Stage of development	Criteria for acceptance
Licensing	Quality Safety Efficacy
Available on NHS	Safety Efficacy Acceptability Cost 'Rationing'
Use by prescribers	Safety Efficacy Acceptability Cost Availability (on formulary, on NHS)

▲ **Fig. 35** Criteria for acceptance of new drugs at different stages of development.

Who decides which drugs should be available for prescription?

Decisions are made at the level of the individual, the institution, the health authority and nationally. At each level, the decision-making process is used to develop a list or set of drugs that will be used in clinical practice.

- Individuals become familiar with a small number of drugs (usually 50–200) that they are comfortable prescribing. New drugs are added to or rejected from this list based on, for example, clinical evidence, anecdotal experience, views of colleagues and marketing pressures.

- Institutions may develop a 'formulary' that lists drugs that are acceptable for prescription in that institution. The aim of the formulary is to promote best practice, by allowing the prescription only of drugs that

are proven to be safe, effective and acceptable. Formularies are also used to try to reduce drug costs for an institution by encouraging prescribing of the cheapest effective drugs for each condition.

- The National Institute for Health and Clinical Excellence (NICE) is a national organisation set up by the government. NICE uses standard criteria of efficacy, safety, acceptability and cost to assess medicines, but also takes into account medical, economic, social and 'moral' perspectives when deciding whether the drug should be available for prescription on the National Health Service.

In practice, decisions about drugs that will be available for prescription are made at all levels, and there are advantages and disadvantages to each (Table 37).

6.3 Clinical governance and rational prescribing

Example 29: A tale of two heart attacks

Patient A

A patient is admitted to hospital with suspected myocardial infarction (MI). Immediately on arrival the diagnosis is confirmed by ECG, he is given 300 mg of aspirin to chew and thrombolysis is started within 20 minutes of his coming through the door of the Emergency Department. He is transferred to the coronary care unit (CCU), where he receives a statin, beta-blockers and an angiotensin-converting enzyme inhibitor, as well as continuing with aspirin. These treatments continue on discharge.

Decision-making level	Advantages	Disadvantages
TABLE 37 DECISION-MAKING AND RATIONAL PRESCRIBING		
Individual prescriber	In touch with patients needs If individual makes the decision, he or she is more likely to implement it Process of critical appraisal helps with continued education	Insufficient time available for detailed appraisal required Inefficient if same process is repeated by, for example, 100,000 doctors Responsibility for decisions about, for example, cost may interfere with doctor–patient relationship Individual decisions heavily influenced by personal bias
Institution (hospital or primary care group)	Decisions relevant to local needs Local ownership of decisions may improve implementation	Inefficient if same work is repeated in many institutions Inequalities where different institutions reach different decisions
Health authority	Decisions made at distance from prescriber–patient relationship Decision less subject to clinician bias (but more subject to manager bias?)	Inefficient if same work is repeated in many regions Variability leads to 'postcode prescribing' Decisions may not take account of local need Decisions divorced from clinical situation, therefore less likely to be supported or implemented
Government decision on basis of advice from NICE	Decisions made at national level, removing local and regional variability Government can be blamed for the cost of decisions, protecting relationship of healthcare providers with patients Efficient as work needs to be done only once and disseminated to all prescribers	Out of touch with needs of patients and prescribers Slow and bureaucratic Perceived as a threat to autonomy by doctors Subject to change with political climate Subject to economic pressures, eg from pharmaceutical companies which may threaten to withdraw income and jobs, etc.

NICE, National Institute for Health and Clinical Excellence.

Patient B

A patient is admitted to hospital with suspected MI. As the admitting department is exceptionally busy, he waits 4 hours for the ECG to be done and to be reported by the on-call junior physician. The doctor who attends the patient has recently seen a patient die from intracerebral haemorrhage after thrombolysis and is reluctant to give this treatment. Eventually, after discussion with colleagues, thrombolysis is started 6 hours after the patient arrived in hospital and 12 hours after the pain commenced. Aspirin is forgotten in the confusion. The patient is admitted to a medical ward as there are no beds on the CCU. He is not seen during his admission by a senior doctor and is ultimately discharged by the house officer on aspirin and isosorbide mononitrate.

Comment

Patient A receives evidence-based and well-organised treatment. Patient B receives poorly organised treatment in which the evidence has largely been forgotten or ignored.

- What factors could have led to inferior treatment for patient B?
- How can we ensure that more patients receive the best treatment available?

Introduction

Clinical governance has become a catchphrase that is used by many but understood by few. It can be encapsulated by a few simple concepts. It is desirable for every patient to receive the best care available as defined by current evidence. Many factors, some of which are illustrated by patient B, hinder individual patients receiving the best possible care, including the following:

- practitioners lack knowledge of best available care;
- practitioners have personal bias for or against bad or good practice;

- practitioners are overstretched and therefore forget, or are unable, to provide the best care possible;
- practitioners may not be motivated to provide best care;
- resources are not available (eg beds, drugs, staff and theatre time) to provide best care.

Clinical governance describes a symbiotic relationship between individuals and institutions, which attempts to overcome these factors and enable good medical practice and high standards of care to be achieved. The individual accepts responsibility to work in a way that is compatible with the values and strategic objectives of the organisation (eg hospital or primary care trust). The organisation takes responsibility for the provision of appropriate facilities for medical work and support of professional development of practitioners and clinical teams on a continuing basis.

The process of clinical governance

The process of clinical governance involves the following.

- setting standards, eg by evidence-based guidelines and protocols;
- monitoring standards, eg by clinical audit, risk assessment, patient survey, complaint and critical incident monitoring;
- maintaining standards through implementation of necessary improvements identified by monitoring, eg through staff education, training and development, and through implementation of new research findings.

Clinical governance can make a huge contribution to ensuring that the prescribing of medicines in clinical practice is done effectively, safely, acceptably and cost-effectively. Some examples are shown below:

Setting standards

- Formularies can be used to define drugs that are effective, safe, acceptable and cost-effective.
- Best prescribing practice, as assessed by available evidence, can be incorporated into guidelines.
- Guidelines within institutions can include drug doses and methods of administration to reduce prescribing errors.
- National guidelines (eg NICE) and independent drug reviews (eg *Drug and Therapeutics Bulletin*, *Prescriber's Journal*) can help determine the place of drugs in therapy.

Monitoring standards

- Clinical audit of prescribing practice can ensure that guidelines and formularies are adhered to and that prescribing is cost-effective.
- Monitoring of adverse drug reactions and prescribing errors can be used to assess and limit risk.
- Patient surveys can be performed to determine drug acceptability.

Maintaining standards

- Drugs and therapeutics committees can assess new drugs that enter the market.
- A regular update of guidelines should include the place of new drugs in treatment, and there should be regular review of older medicines.
- There should be training and education of all practitioners in the principles of rational prescribing and critical appraisal, which might be performed by clinical pharmacologists and clinical pharmacists.

How can clinical governance help?

Clinical governance can help to overcome some of the problems that led to patient B receiving unsatisfactory treatment for his MI. In theory the use of many aspects of clinical governance should ensure that:

- patients with chest pain are treated as priority and receive an immediate ECG, which is reported without delay;

- patients receive thrombolysis according to need, irrespective of an individual practitioner's bias;

- 'door-to-needle time' is minimised to ensure that thrombolysis is given as quickly as possible;

- standard treatment guidelines (based on evidence) are followed, so that treatment is not forgotten even when busy (aspirin) or when the practitioner is not personally aware of current evidence (discharge medication).

In this case, it was also the responsibility of the individual physician in charge to review the patient regularly and to ensure implementation of good medical practice and the responsibility of the institution to provide, for example, adequate staff to see urgent patients more quickly and adequate facilities such as CCU beds.

6.4 Rational prescribing: evaluating the evidence for yourself

Not all new therapies are inevitably better than older ones: while new drugs are under patent protection they are likely to be more expensive

and will not carry the same safety reassurance that arises from the long-term use of an agent in routine clinical practice. Doctors and (increasingly) patients are bombarded with new information on the apparent benefits of the latest therapies. The reliability of such information, from sources ranging from the lay media and World Wide Web to specialist medical and scientific journals, is extremely variable.

A number of publications provide excellent and largely unbiased distillations of the evidence on a new drug or disease management. These are usually directed at doctors (eg *Drug and Therapeutics Bulletin* in the UK, as well as *Clinical Evidence*), but some (eg *Best Treatments*) are targeted at patients. The National Institute for Health and Clinical Excellence (NICE) also bases its guidance on information obtained from high-quality clinical trials of new drugs where possible. However, because some of the sources of information on new treatments may be prone to certain biases that might diminish their utility for guiding prescribing (particularly information directed at a lay audience or materials distributed to doctors as part of the marketing of a new drug), there is no substitute for developing a few key skills that will enable you to evaluate the available evidence for yourself. When met with the cry of 'where's the evidence' – an increasingly common refrain on the medical ward round – you should be in a position to discuss the pros and cons of a new therapy and use this judgement to the benefit of your patients.

6.5 Rational prescribing, irrational patients

Example 30: Living in the 'real world'

You review a 55-year-old man in a general medical clinic who has hypertension and type 2 diabetes. He has been prescribed lisinopril 10 mg once daily. His blood pressure is 180/110 mmHg and he has proteinuria. His creatinine is 200 μmol/L. On close questioning, he admits that he has not taken any of the tablets.

- Why might patients not take prescribed medication?
- What are the implications for this patient in not taking antihypertensive medication?
- How might you approach the consultation?

Patients not taking the prescribed medication

As many as 50% of people with chronic illness do not take their medication in optimal doses and so do not derive the optimal benefits of treatment. This is true even where the consequences of not taking treatment may be life-threatening. For example, about 22% of recipients of renal transplants miss doses of immunosuppressive medication and 60–70% of patients with HIV omit doses of antiretroviral therapy.

Failure to take prescribed medication and its impact on health

Non-adherence to, or non-compliance with, treatment has considerable health and economic costs for both individuals and society. Non-adherence to prescribed treatment contributes significantly to premature death from many conditions, including asthma, cardiovascular disease, epilepsy and diabetes. Non-adherence increases morbidity, which increases requirements for healthcare and results in lost working days and reduced productivity. Non-adherence to antituberculous medication or antibiotics may lead to the spread of infection or the emergence of resistant organisms, which endanger other members of society.

Reasons for non-adherence to treatment

There are many reasons why patients do not take prescribed medication. Common reasons include the following:

- lack of confidence in the efficacy of medicines or in the advice of doctors;

- perception that medication is unnecessary;

- intolerance of side effects;

- fear of ill effects of medication over time, eg addiction or immunity to medicines, or the development of cancer;

- experiences or advice from relatives or friends regarding the medication;

- stigma attached to taking treatment, eg for HIV, tuberculosis or mental illness;

- difficulty taking medication in daily routine or forgetting to take medication;

- lack of information about medicines or inability to understand which medicines to take and when.

Impact of the prescribing encounter

The relationship between doctor and patient and the quality of the 'prescribing encounter' can have a substantial impact on the likelihood that the patient will take the prescribed medication. Several different models of medical encounters have been described.

- Paternalistic prescribing encounter: the doctor decides what treatment to implement, informs the patient of this choice and its implications, and prescribes the drug. The patient is compliant (or non-compliant) with treatment.

- Shared model: the doctor and patient share medical and other relevant information, and participate in all stages of the decision-making process simultaneously. The prescription is the outcome of joint deliberation. The doctor and patient reach agreement (concordance) on the treatment to be tried.

It is expected (but not unequivocally proven) that the shared model would improve adherence to treatment by enabling the patient to discuss beliefs and fears when starting new medication and to have some ownership in the decision to take the drug. Concordance allows that the view of the patient is as important as, if not more important than, the doctor's view in making the prescribing decision. The decision not to take treatment is therefore perfectly valid, providing it is made in the light of full and accurate information.

Example 30: Living in the 'real world' (*continued*)

Clinical approach

This patient has renal impairment with hypertension and type 2 diabetes mellitus. Control of his BP is essential to slow further deterioration of his renal function, as well as to reduce his risk of vascular disease. A lecture on the stupidity of not taking tablets is unlikely to make any difference to his adherence to treatment and may deter him from attending for further follow-up appointments. Ideally, discussion in the consultation will explore the knowledge, attitudes and beliefs of both doctor and patient, which include:

- the nature and severity of the patient's illness;
- the patient's reasons for taking or not taking medication;
- the feasibility of the proposed treatment regimen.

Negotiation around these issues may lead to the patient deciding to take the tablets.

FURTHER READING

Embracing patient partnership (themed issue). *BMJ* 1999; 319 (No. 7212): available at http://www.bmj.com/content/vol319/issue7212/

7.1 Self-assessment questions

Question 1

A 54-year-old woman with chronic mild renal impairment (serum creatinine 160 µmol/L) is admitted to hospital with palpitations. She is found to have fast atrial fibrillation with a ventricular rate of 140 bpm. A decision is made to control her ventricular rate with digoxin and she is started on warfarin. Which one of the following statements is true?

Answers

A Digoxin undergoes extensive hepatic metabolism

B Digoxin is absolutely contraindicated in the presence of renal impairment

C The loading dose of digoxin should be reduced due to her renal impairment

D The maintenance dose of digoxin should be reduced due to her renal impairment

E The loading dose of warfarin should be reduced due to her renal impairment

Question 2

A 34-year-old woman who is 8 weeks' pregnant requires antihypertensive therapy. Which one of the following drugs should definitely *not* be given?

Answers

A Methyldopa

B Labetalol

C Nifedipine

D Losartan

E Hydralazine

Question 3

A 24-year-old woman who is 12 weeks' pregnant presents with cellulitis of her leg. She has no known drug allergies. Which one of the following antibiotics should definitely *not* be given?

Answers

A Flucloxacillin

B Ceftriaxone

C Co-trimoxazole

D Benzylpenicillin

E Erythromycin

Question 4

A 36-year-old woman is currently taking several medications and wonders whether they would be safe if she was breast-feeding her baby. Which one of the following drugs is *not* considered to be safe in breast-feeding?

Answers

A Warfarin

B Phenoxymethylpenicillin

C Digoxin

D Aspirin

E Insulin

Question 5

A 55-year-old man is started on digoxin for atrial fibrillation. Which of the following measurements would be most useful when monitoring him for digoxin efficacy?

Answers

A Blood pressure

B Glomerular filtration rate

C Plasma digoxin concentration

D Pulse rate

E Urea and creatinine

Question 6

A 77-year-old man on warfarin for venous thromboembolic disease is admitted with a second deep vein thrombosis despite taking warfarin. His INR is 1.2. Which of the following medicines when co-administered with warfarin is most likely to have caused this clinical picture?

Answers

A Aspirin

B Cimetidine

C Cholestyramine

D Cyproterone acetate

E Erythromycin

Question 7

A 23-year-old man requires antibiotic therapy. Which of the following is the strongest indication for using an intravenous route of administration?

Answers

A Antibiotics have previously given him severe diarrhoea

B He has a temperature of 39°C and a white cell count of 21×10^9/L (normal range 4–11)

C The antibiotic has a short plasma half-life

D The antibiotic is recycled by the enterohepatic circulation

E The most suitable antibiotic is highly water soluble

Question 8

A 66-year-old woman who requires treatment with amiodarone for intractable arrhythmias is given an intravenous loading dose of 300 mg (5 mg/kg). Which of the following best explains why a loading dose is used in this patient?

Answers

A Amiodarone clearance is genetically determined

B Amiodarone has a long plasma half-life

C Amiodarone is eliminated by zero-order metabolism

D Amiodarone is rapidly metabolised by the liver

E Amiodarone is widely bound in body tissues

Question 9

A 55-year-old man with liver failure is on a number of medications. Which of the following will be less effective as a result of his illness?

Answers

A Diazepam

B Enalapril

C Spironolactone

D Paracetamol

E Warfarin

Question 10

A 22-year-old man has a creatinine clearance of 90 mL/min but penicillin clearance of 360 mL/min. This means that:

Answers

A His creatinine production is reduced due to muscle disease

B He has received a recent dose of probenecid

C His glomerular filtration rate is increased by antibiotic therapy

D Penicillin is more lipid soluble than creatinine

E Penicillin is secreted into the urine by the renal tubules

Question 11

A 36-year-old man is brought to the Emergency Department following

significant trauma. He is in pain and is appropriately given 10 mg of morphine as a bolus intravenously. A few minutes later he develops facial flushing, wheezing and his BP falls. Which of the following is *not* a feature of an anaphylactoid reaction?

Answers

A Urticaria

B Histamine release

C IgE-mediated mast cell degranulation

D Bronchospasm

E Anxiety

Question 12

Which of the following is *not* true of metformin therapy?

Answers

A It is unsafe in acute porphyria

B It can cause a lactic acidosis

C It seldom causes hypoglycaemia

D It should be avoided in severe hepatic dysfunction

E Toxicity is more likely with renal impairment

Question 13

A 43-year-old woman presents to her doctor with a raised, non-blanching and purpuric rash, which is mainly on her lower limbs. She has recently been started on a new medication for hypertension. Which of the following drugs is she most likely to have been prescribed?

Answers

A Atenolol

B Amlodipine

C Hydralazine

D Diltiazem

E Ramipril

Question 14

A 24-year-old woman presents with headache, neck stiffness and photophobia. You are concerned about possible bacterial meningitis.

The letter from the GP records significant penicillin allergy. Which of the following is true of patients with allergy to penicillin?

Answers

A They have a 30% chance of cross-reacting to a cephalosporin

B They can safely be treated with meropenem

C They can present with haemolytic anaemia

D T cells are not involved in the allergic reaction

E Reactions occur within 4 hours of administration

Question 15

A 72-year-old man with known chronic obstructive pulmonary disease and epilepsy is admitted with a severe community-acquired pneumonia and a urinary tract infection. He is taking an antiepileptic and a tablet for 'wheeze'. He is given high-dose intravenous penicillin, erythromycin and ciprofloxacin. On the ward round the next morning he has a self-terminating grand mal seizure. Which of the following is *least* likely to have precipitated his seizure?

Answers

A Penicillin

B Erythromycin, by increasing levels of theophylline

C Erythromycin, by lowering levels of carbamazepine

D Ciprofloxacin

E Sepsis

Question 16

A 56-year-old man is taking azathioprine as a steroid-sparing medication for Crohn's disease. He presents to his doctor with an acutely tender first metatarsal joint. He is prescribed allopurinol and colchicine. Three weeks later he is admitted with a fever and his white cell count is found to be 1.1×10^9/L.

Which of the following are *not* recognised causes of agranulocytosis?

Answers

A Co-trimoxazole

B Colchicine

C Clozapine

D Carbimazole

E Induction of xanthine oxidase by allopurinol

Question 17

A 72-year-old man has been on amiodarone 200 mg a day for several years for control of atrial fibrillation. At his regular cardiology outpatient appointment he is noted to have slate-grey discoloration of the face. Which of the following adverse effects is *not* associated with amiodarone therapy?

Answers

A Glaucoma

B Corneal microdeposits

C Photosensitivity

D Thyroid-stimulating hormone (TSH) >20 mU/L with low T_4

E Elevated T_3 and suppressed TSH

Question 18

A 29-year-old woman is started on quadruple antituberculous medication (rifampicin, isoniazid, ethambutol and pyrazinamide). Which of the following is *not* true with regard to antituberculous therapy?

Answers

A Colour vision should be tested prior to starting ethambutol

B Peripheral neuropathy with isoniazid is more common in slow acetylators

C Peripheral neuropathy with isoniazid can be prevented with pyridoxine (vitamin B_6)

D Isoniazid-induced hepatitis is more common in slow acetylators

E Rifampicin reduces the efficacy of the oral contraceptive pill

Question 19

Which of the following is *not* true of drug-induced haemolytic anaemia?

Answers

A It can be associated with a positive direct or indirect Coombs' test

B It can be caused by methyldopa

C The mechanism can involve autoantibody formation or complement activation by immune complexes

D It only occurs in patients with glucose-6-phosphate dehydrogenase deficiency

E It can be caused by quinidine

Question 20

A 76-year-old man with rheumatoid arthritis and atrial fibrillation presents with a 5-day history of shortness of breath, cough and decreased exercise tolerance. A CXR shows unilateral alveolar infiltrates and lung biopsy reveals acute eosinophilic pneumonia. Which of the following of his medications could account for his condition?

Answers

A Digoxin

B Sulfasalazine

C Ciprofloxacin

D Atenolol

E Paracetamol

7.2 Self-assessment answers

Answer to Question 1

D

Digoxin is excreted by the kidneys and does not undergo significant hepatic metabolism. Digoxin can be used in the presence of renal impairment, but its clearance is impaired in the presence of reduced renal function and therefore the maintenance dose of digoxin should be reduced. The loading dose of digoxin is unchanged. Therapeutic drug monitoring of digoxin levels may be useful in guiding therapy. Warfarin undergoes mainly hepatic metabolism and the loading dose does not need to be adjusted in renal impairment.

Answer to Question 2

D

Losartan is an angiotensin receptor antagonist. Angiotensin-converting enzyme inhibitors and angiotensin receptor antagonists both have fetotoxic effects, including renal agenesis and oligohydramnios, and are contraindicated in pregnancy. Methyldopa, labetalol and hydralazine have a long record of safe use in pregnancy. Although there are some concerns about nifedipine inhibiting labour, it is generally regarded as safe for use in pregnancy.

Answer to Question 3

C

Co-trimoxazole is the combination of sulfamethoxazole and trimethoprim. Trimethoprim is a folate antagonist and is teratogenic so should not be used in pregnancy. The other drugs listed are generally considered safe for use in pregnancy.

Answer to Question 4

D

Aspirin is not considered to be safe in breast-feeding due to the risk of causing Reye's syndrome in the baby. Whether a drug is safe in breast-feeding depends both on how much of the drug enters the breast milk and on the toxicity of those levels to the baby. The other drugs listed either pass into breast milk in very small amounts or are considered to be non-toxic to the baby.

Answer to Question 5

D

You wish to monitor efficacy of digoxin, which is used for rate control in atrial fibrillation. Blood pressure will give some measure of cardiac function but will not give as much information as pulse rate. Measuring drug plasma concentration will tell you whether digoxin is at therapeutic concentrations in the blood, but not whether it is having a therapeutic effect. Urea, creatinine and glomerular filtration rate will give an indication of renal function and likely clearance (but not efficacy) of digoxin.

Answer to Question 6

C

Cholestyramine can reduce warfarin absorption, thereby preventing effective anticoagulation and lowering of the INR. The INR would be *increased* by co-prescription of cimetidine and erythromycin, which are cytochrome P450 inhibitors. Cyproterone acetate (an antiandrogen used for prostate cancer) carries a risk of recurrence of thromboembolic disease but would not alter the INR. Aspirin inhibits cyclooxygenase and prostaglandin production and increases the risk of bleeding in a patient receiving warfarin, but it would not affect the INR.

Answer to Question 7

E

Water-soluble drugs (eg aminoglycosides) are poorly absorbed across lipid membranes and therefore will not be absorbed when given orally; hence a parenteral route of administration is essential. Temperature and white cell count mark the inflammatory response, not necessarily the severity of infection, and antibiotic-associated diarrhoea can occur when antibiotics are given by oral or parenteral routes. Aminoglycosides have a short half-life and for this reason some physicians give them intramuscularly once daily to delay absorption and increase the time the drug is in circulation, instead of intravenous administration three times daily. Recirculation by the enterohepatic circulation could contribute to the plasma drug concentration, but does not require intravenous administration.

Answer to Question 8

E

Tissue-binding sites must be 'filled up' by a loading dose before a therapeutic plasma concentration can be achieved. Metabolism/elimination/clearance rates and plasma half-life determine the time taken to achieve a steady-state plasma concentration and the level of that steady-state concentration when a steady dosing regimen is established.

Answer to Question 9

B

Enalapril is a prodrug and requires metabolism to enalaprilat by the liver for activation. Diazepam is also metabolised by the liver to an active metabolite. However, diazepam itself is active and liver failure will delay the elimination of diazepam as well as warfarin, thereby increasing their activity. Paracetamol activity will be unaffected by liver failure, although its metabolism will be reduced and

the *British National Formulary* advises avoidance of large doses. Aldosterone metabolism is reduced in liver failure, causing salt and water retention and contributing to ascites and oedema, which can be treated by spironolactone.

Answer to Question 10

E

The plasma clearance (mL/min) measures the volume of blood (mL) from which a substance (here creatinine or penicillin) has been cleared in 1 minute. The glomerular filtration rate (GFR) is normally 90–120 mL/min in men, and as creatinine is filtered and mostly not secreted or reabsorbed by the renal tubules, then this volume of blood is cleared of creatinine in 1 minute. Penicillin is secreted in the renal tube and this is added to the amount that is filtered, raising the volume of blood that is cleared of penicillin beyond the GFR. These results are normal and do not imply muscle or renal disease. Lipid solubility would reduce plasma clearance of a drug by increasing tubular reabsorption. Probenecid would prevent secretion of penicillin by the renal tubules, reducing drug clearance.

Answer to Question 11

C

An anaphylactoid reaction is clinically indistinguishable from a type 1 hypersensitivity reaction and acute management is the same. Both reactions involve the release of histamine from mast cells and basophils; in anaphylactoid reaction, this is not mediated by the binding of IgE to drug antigens but rather by the direct action of the drug on mast cells leading to mediator release. The same mechanism underlies the 'red-man' syndrome associated with rapid infusion of vancomycin.

NSAIDs, radio-opaque contrast media and progesterone can also cause an anaphylactoid reaction. The incriminated drug may be used again, but at a lower dose or at a lower rate of administration. Other adverse effects of opioid analgesics include nausea and vomiting, constipation, urinary retention, confusion and respiratory depression.

Answer to Question 12

A

Sulphonylureas (tolbutamide and chlorpropamide) are considered unsafe in porphyria, but metformin is considered safe. Lactic acidosis with metformin is an uncommon but serious adverse effect that is more likely to occur in renal impairment. Metformin sensitises cells to insulin, promotes glucose uptake, suppresses the hepatic release of glucose and is largely ineffective in the complete absence of insulin. It is rarely associated with hypoglycaemia, unlike insulin and other oral hypoglycaemics. Impaired liver function increases the risks associated with lactic acidosis, since lactate cannot be cleared by the liver.

Answer to Question 13

C

Purpura in the context of a drug reaction may be an isolated skin reaction, or it may be a manifestation of drug-induced thrombocytopenia or drug-induced vasculitis. Hydralazine is associated with drug-induced lupus-like syndrome that can present with a vasculitic purpuric rash. Systemic features such as fever, malaise and arthralgia may be present, and other organs including the liver, kidney and heart may be affected. Anti-histone antibodies may also be present. The drug should be stopped

immediately and systemic corticosteroids may be of benefit. Other drugs associated with a purpuric skin rash include aspirin, sulphonamides, penicillin, thiazides, furosemide and corticosteroids.

Answer to Question 14

C

The rate of cross-reaction with cephalosporins is between 5 and 10%; they should still be avoided in a patient with a clear history of β-lactam allergy. Cross-reactivity with meropenem and imipenem is around 10% and an alternative should be used unless skin testing to penicillin is known to be negative. Haemolytic anaemia does occur, particularly after long-term treatment at high doses (type II reaction). T cells mediate the maculopapular rash (type IV reaction) associated with penicillin therapy. Even type I reactions to penicillin can occur as late as 72 hours after therapy. Always take a detailed history regarding possible penicillin allergy and take advice on alternatives: chloramphenicol, vancomycin and rifampicin may be reasonable therapy for bacterial meningitis in a truly penicillin-allergic patient.

Answer to Question 15

C

Penicillins, imipenem, ciprofloxacin and metronidazole have all been associated with a lowering of the seizure threshold. Intercurrent sepsis could also account for his seizure. Erythromycin *increases* the levels of carbamazepine via inhibition of cytochrome P450, and hence carbamazepine toxicity can result and seizures may occur. Increases in serum levels of theophylline occur with erythromycin therapy and can cause seizures. Inhibition of cytochrome

P450 by erythromycin can also lead to an enhanced anticoagulation effect with warfarin and an increased incidence of rhabdomyolysis with statin therapy. Always obtain an accurate drug history and consider possible interactions when prescribing.

Answer to Question 16

E

Allopurinol inhibits xanthine oxidase and leads to the accumulation of azathioprine metabolites that cause bone marrow suppression. All the others are recognised causes of agranulocytosis. Colchicine more commonly causes gastrointestinal adverse effects (bloating and diarrhoea). Patients taking clozapine, carbimazole and propylthiouracil for hyperthyroidism should have regular monitoring of blood counts during therapy and be told to report any symptoms of infection early.

Answer to Question 17

A

Amiodarone is a highly effective and useful antiarrhythmic agent, but using it for long-term therapy is associated with a diverse list of adverse effects. As well as pulmonary toxicity the important adverse effects include thyroid, hepatic, cardiac, neurological, skin, ocular and gastrointestinal toxicity. Adverse effects of amiodarone on the thyroid either arise from the effect of iodine overload (a daily dose of 200 mg of amiodarone provides approximately 25 times the daily recommended intake of iodine) or from direct toxic effect of the drug on the thyroid gland. Hypothyroidism occurs in up to 10% of amiodarone-treated patients. Low T_3 levels may occur in euthyroid patients on amiodarone, and diagnosis is based on an elevated TSH above 20 mU/L with a low T_4 in association with appropriate clinical features. It can be successfully treated with thyroxine, so discontinuation of amiodarone is not necessarily required. Hyperthyrodism associated with amiodarone can be due to a destructive thyroiditis with release of excess thyroid hormones. Alternatively, it could be caused by the unmasking of subclinical underlying thyroid disease such as multinodular or diffuse goitre, where the excess iodine load leads to excess hormone synthesis. Thyroid function tests and liver function tests (amiodarone causes a transaminitis in up to 20% of patients) should be checked at baseline and every 3–6 months while on therapy. Skin reactions to amiodarone include blue-grey skin pigmentation and photosensitivity. Glaucoma can be precipitated by corticosteroids (open-angle mechanism) or in susceptible individuals by drugs causing pupillary dilatation (closed-angle mechanism): these include topical anticholinergic or sympathomimetic dilating drops, tricyclic antidepressants and antiparkinsonian drugs.

Answer to Question 18

D

Slow acetylators have higher circulating levels of isoniazid which makes them more susceptible to peripheral neuropathy and means dose adjustment is required. In contrast, fast acetylators are at greater risk of isoniazid-induced hepatitis. Ethambutol causes an optic neuritis that can be detected by changes in colour vision; testing should be performed at baseline and at regular intervals during therapy, and the risk is increased in patients with renal impairment. Rifampicin is the classic example of a hepatic enzyme inducer. Always check co-prescriptions of patients prescribed rifampicin and advise them appropriately; for instance, rifampicin can induce the metabolism of corticosteroids and so their dose may need to be doubled or even quadrupled during rifampicin treatment.

Answer to Question 19

D

A direct antiglobulin test (DAT) or Coombs' test detects IgG or C3 bound to the red cell membrane. A positive DAT is seen when drugs cause IgG or complement to bind to red cells. Addition of Coombs' reagent (a mixture of anti-human IgG and anti-human complement) to red cells causes red cell agglutination and confirms the immune aetiology. An indirect Coombs' test looks for anti-red cell antibodies in serum. It can be positive if the drug is included in the incubation. A drug-induced haemolysis can be truly autoimmune with the development of anti-red cell antibodies (methyldopa, levodopa and procainamide); it can also be a consequence of immune complex formation (quinine, quinidine and isoniazid); or it can occur via the formation of drug–hapten complexes on red cells that are recognised as foreign antigens (penicillins and cephalosporins). Drug-induced haemolysis is most often associated with glucose-6-phosphate dehydrogenase (G6PD) deficiency, but not exclusively. In G6PD deficiency the haemolysis is due to the oxidative stress rather than an autoimmune phenomenon.

Answer to Question 20

B

Long-term sulfasalazine therapy is sometimes associated with pulmonary toxicity that presents as dyspnoea with pulmonary infiltrates. More commonly it causes gastrointestinal upset and nausea. Leucopenia, rash and abnormal results in liver function tests also occur. Pulmonary toxicity also occurs with amiodarone, nitrofurantoin, NSAIDs, methotrexate, bleomycin (fibrotic picture) and other chemotherapeutic agents (taxanes and gemcitabine). Withdrawal of the offending drug and steroid therapy are the mainstays of treatment.

STATISTICS, EPIDEMIOLOGY, CLINICAL TRIALS AND META-ANALYSES

Authors:

J Danesh and CJM Whitty

Editor:

JD Firth

Editor-in-Chief:

JD Firth

Statistics is a large subject. Fortunately, physicians have to understand only a limited number of statistical techniques to conduct and understand the vast majority of clinical studies. These techniques are simple and well worth mastering. The hard work will almost always be done by a computer, so it is rather like driving: you do not have to know how a car works, but you do need to know how to steer it.

Continuous and categorical variables

Data are broadly divided into two categories.

- Continuous variables: data that can incorporate a whole range of values, eg age, BP, temperature and blood glucose.
- Categorical variables: data that fall into a few clearly defined categories, eg dead or alive, male or female, or white, south Asian or Afro-Caribbean.

Continuous data are often turned into categorical data to guide clinical practice, for example we categorise BP into hypertensive or normotensive, or the blood glucose response as diabetic, glucose intolerant or normal. These divisions are often arbitrary, but we use them for clinical decision-making all the time.

Descriptive statistics

Continuous data

For statistical purposes continuous data have to be subdivided, as shown in Fig. 1, into:

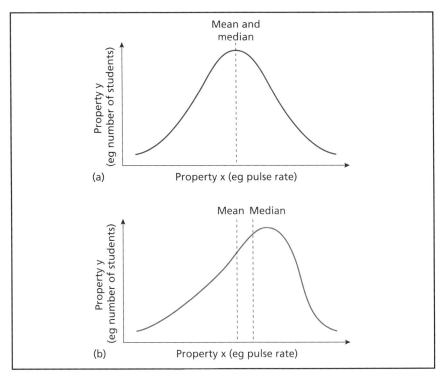

▲ **Fig. 1** (a) Normally distributed and (b) skewed data.

- normal distribution;

- skewed distribution.

This is far more important than is sometimes realised, because it defines how the data should be described and tested from then on. Often this is the only statistical decision you need to make. Central to this is the difference between the mean and the median. If a group of 251 students had their pulse taken, the mean is the sum of all the pulses divided by the number of students (and this may be a fraction, eg 76.6). The median is the pulse rate of the student who is in the middle of the group if they are all lined up in order from the lowest to the highest (and will always be a whole

number). In normally distributed data, the mean and median are about the same.

Normally distributed data

Normally distributed data are best summarised using the mean and standard deviation (SD), eg a study will quote 'mean age 34.6, SD 5.6 years'). Statistical tests on normally distributed data also use the mean. The problem is that the mean will be wildly misleading if the data are highly skewed. If we did a study of alcohol intake sampling 100 medical students, the median alcohol intake might be 12 units per week. But a few keen members of a drinking club could easily push the mean up to 30 or more without affecting the median.

TABLE 1 DESCRIBING AND TESTING DATA

Data type	Describe with	To test two groups
Categorical data	Percentage or proportion	Chi-squared (χ^2)
Normally distributed continuous	Mean and standard deviation	Student's t-test
Skewed continuous	Median and range	Wilcoxon rank-sum test/Mann–Whitney U-test

> ⚠ Using the mean to describe seriously skewed data will be misleading, and statistical tests using the mean will be uninterpretable.

Skewed data Skewed data should always be summarised using the median, and statistical analysis requires different tests that use the median. The range is usually quoted (rather than the SD, which is based on the mean), for example 'median age 24, range 16–55'.

> 🔑 How do you decide whether data are skewed or not?
>
> Generally, the best way is to plot it out and look at it! However, a reasonable rule of thumb is that data are skewed when the mean and median are more than slightly different.

Categorical data

Categorical data fall into neat blocks and are usually summarised using percentages (eg 54% of the group were women, 46% were men).

Statistical tests of association

Most clinical studies are interested in whether there is a difference between one group and one or more others, eg comparing BP in those with or without a stroke, or whether drug A leads to fewer deaths than drug B. Statistical tests are designed to find out whether the difference between one group and another may have

arisen by chance alone. Formally they test the null hypothesis, namely that there is no difference between one group and another.

Once we have decided whether data are categorical or continuous, and if continuous whether they are skewed or normally distributed, the correct statistical technique to use automatically follows. There is no magic to this. Table 1 compares the different methods of summarising and testing categorical, normally distributed and skewed data.

Categorical variable against categorical variable

Say we wish to compare two groups of categorical data, eg dead/alive by drug/placebo. For looking at one categorical variable against another, the correct test is chi-squared (χ^2). Data are put into a 2 × 2 (or 2 × 3 or 2 × 4) table, and a χ^2 statistic calculated.

There is a quick formula for calculating χ^2 for a 2 × 2 table. To do this, without a computer, consider the example of the effect of a drug on death in Table 2, where:

$$\chi^2 = n(ad - bc)^2/efgh$$

The χ^2 statistic does not, in itself, mean anything concrete to the reader, but does allow a P value to be read off a statistical table (see below). For a 2 × 2 table, there are two degrees of freedom; for anything more leave it to the computer.

> ⚠ Chi-squared (and its variations) is probably the single most widely used test in medicine, particularly in clinical trials. Therefore it is worth being aware of a couple of pitfalls.
>
> - If you construct your table and there are less than five in any one box, then simple χ^2 may be invalid and you will probably need a variant called Fisher's exact test, which is slightly more rigorous.
> - If you have a zero in any box, seek statistical help as χ^2 may not be valid at all.

Chi-squared can also be used to look for trends where there is a logical sequence of categories. You might be interested in the prevalence of angina in doctors you have divided

TABLE 2 EFFECTS OF DRUGS A AND B ON PATIENT DEATH. CALCULATION OF THE χ^2 STATISTIC FOR A 2 × 2 TABLE: SEE TEXT FOR EXPLANATION

	Drug A	Drug B	
Dead	a	b	$e\ (a + b)$
Alive	c	d	$f\ (c + d)$
	$g\ (a + c)$	$h\ (b + d)$	n (total)

into thin, medium and fat; there is a variation of χ^2 (χ^2 for trend) that can test for this. It is, however, easy to misuse, so seek statistical help.

Categorical variable against normally distributed continuous variable

For comparing a normally distributed continuous variable between two categorical groups, we almost invariably use Student's *t*-test. Examples might be comparing BP in a group on bendroflumethiazide and a group on captopril. The *t*-test calculates a statistic from which a *P* value is derived. The *t*-test is robust, provided that the data are normally distributed. Tests on normally distributed data are also known as parametric tests.

Categorical variable against skewed continuous variable

When comparing data from two groups that are skewed, we use non-parametric (also known as distribution-free) tests. This will usually be the Wilcoxon rank-sum test (or Mann–Whitney *U*-test).

This is exceptionally laborious to do by hand, but easy for computers. It uses the median as its starting point. Again, a statistic is calculated from which a *P* value is derived. As it is now just as easy to do non-parametric tests as parametric ones, it is reasonable to ask why these are not done in all cases. The reason is that the tests are less powerful and therefore more likely to miss a true difference. So, provided that continuous data are normally distributed, Student's *t*-test is preferable.

Continuous variable against continuous variable

In basic science, it may be necessary to compare one continuous variable against another (eg BP against age) and this is usually done by one

of a variety of regression methods. However, the output is often extremely difficult to summarise or interpret, even for those who have a firm grasp of the mathematics. It is worth knowing that these methods exist, but it is far better to reduce one variable to a categorical variable for studies that are meant to be interpreted by clinicians. Basing clinical decisions on the output of a regression analysis is usually difficult or impossible.

P values and confidence intervals

P values

All the tests quoted (χ^2, Student's *t*-test and Wilcoxon rank-sum) calculate a statistic from which a summary statistic, the *P* value, is derived. The *P* value is a measure of how likely a difference is to have arisen by chance alone.

However it is derived, the *P* value represents the same thing: the probability that an association could have arisen by chance. A *P* value of 0.5 means that there is a 50% chance that the difference is by chance alone, a *P* of 0.07 a 7% chance, and so on. Traditionally, a *P* value of less than 0.05 (5% probability) has been taken as meaning it has not arisen by chance alone, but this is arbitrary.

P values

Two things must be clearly understood about a *P* value.

1. The *P* value does not measure clinical or biological importance: it is not a direct measure of the clinical relevance of any effect and depends crucially on the size of a study. A very large study or meta-analysis can generate very small *P* values for very small (and possibly clinically unimportant) differences, whereas a small study may fail to show

an effect even if there is a large difference between one group and another.
2. The more times one looks at the data, the smaller the *P* value that should be considered important: the conventional cut-off *P* value of 0.05 (a 1 in 20 probability of arising by chance alone) applies only if a single question is asked. If you test the data in lots of different ways (say 20 tests) or at many different time points, one of them will very possibly produce a *P* value of less than 0.05 by chance alone. Statistical techniques are available to make explicit allowance for multiple testing of the same data (eg Bonferonni correction).

Confidence intervals

P values are a reasonable summary, but a more informative way of describing data and seeing how likely a difference is to have arisen by chance alone is the confidence interval (CI). This provides essentially the same information as the *P* value, but is easier to understand and with computers just as easy to calculate.

Formally, the 95% CI around a value is the range within which there is a 95% chance that the true value lies. Similarly, the 95% CI around a difference is the range in which there is a 95% chance that the true difference lies. The top value is the highest value it is likely to be; the bottom value is the lowest value. Confidence intervals can be quoted but they can also be drawn (sometimes informally called 'error bars') on a graph. This makes the concept much easier to understand (Fig. 2).

Assessing significant difference

P values and CIs help to determine whether there is a statistically significant difference between two groups. They do not, however, provide a useful measure of how large or important that difference is.

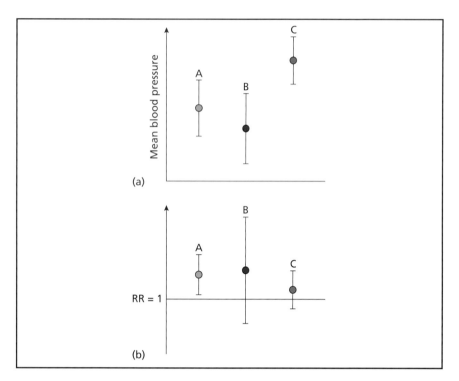

▲ **Fig. 2** Confidence level error bars. (**a**) 95% CIs around mean BP in three groups. Where the CIs overlap, there will be no significant difference. C is significantly different from B, but not from A. (**b**) The 95% CIs around a relative risk (RR) for those given a new drug. Where they cross 1, there is no significant difference. Drug A has a significantly different effect. Drug B has a larger, but non-significant, effect.

In clinical studies four measures are commonly used to do this:

- absolute risk reduction;
- risk ratio;
- odds ratio (OR);
- number needed to treat (NNT).

All these measure the same thing, but express it in different ways. Most clinical studies comparing groups will quote one or more of these parameters, the 95% CI around the value of that parameter and the P value testing whether any difference is statistically significant.

> **Absolute risk reduction (or increase) = Risk in group 1 − Risk in group 2**
>
> **Risk ratio = Risk in group 1/Risk in group 2**
>
> **Odds ratio = Odds in group 1/Odds in group 2**
>
> **Number needed to treat = 1/Absolute risk reduction (or increase)**

Consider the treatment with aspirin of patients who have a myocardial infarction (MI). Let us define risk (of any outcome of interest, eg death) in those given aspirin (exposed) as $p1$ (probability 1) and risk in those not given aspirin (unexposed) as $p0$ (probability 0). Suppose in our example that the death rate is 9.4% in those given aspirin ($p1 = 0.094$) and 11.8% in those not given aspirin ($p0 = 0.118$).

Absolute risk reduction

The absolute risk reduction is the difference of the outcome in one group compared with that in another:

Absolute risk reduction (or increase) $= p0 - p1$

In our example, the absolute risk reduction produced by aspirin is 0.118 − 0.094, or 0.024, meaning that if 100 patients with MI are given aspirin and 100 are not, then there are likely to be two or three more deaths in the 100 not receiving aspirin.

Risk ratio

The risk ratio or relative risk (RR) is simply the ratio of outcome in one group compared with that in another:

RR $= p1/p0$

In our example, there is an RR of death after MI of 0.094/0.118, or 0.80, if you take aspirin. This means that those who took aspirin have 80% of the chance of dying compared with those who did not. Similarly, if you have an RR of 3.0 of developing skin cancer when you sunbathe, this means that three times as many sunbathers develop skin cancer than those who do not sunbathe. As RRs are a simple measure to understand, they are particularly appropriate for clinical trials. An RR of 1 means that there is no difference between two groups.

Odds ratio

The OR is not so intuitive, except to those who understand betting.

OR $= [p1/(1 - p1)]/[p0/(1 - p0)]$

Taking our example again, the OR of dying if given aspirin is (0.094/0.906)/(0.118/0.882), ie 0.1038/0.1338 or 0.78.

As with RR, an OR of 1 means that there is no difference between two groups, and the further we move away from 1 (either up or down) the greater the difference. At small differences (as in our example) OR and RR are roughly the same, but for big differences they become very dissimilar. An RR of 6 means that one group has six times the chance of having a particular outcome; an OR of 6 represents a much smaller difference. The reason OR is widely used despite being less intuitive is that it is easier to handle mathematically, especially when the denominator is not known. The danger with it is that people reading papers often think that a large OR is the same as RR, and they get an exaggerated sense of how big the difference is between one group and another.

Number needed to treat

The clinical significance of a reported reduction in absolute risk, RR or OR is not always obvious. The concept of NNT was devised to make this more obvious, enabling interpretation in terms of patients treated rather than the less intuitive probabilities.

NNT = 1/Absolute risk reduction
$= 1/(p0 - p1)$

In our example the NNT is 1/0.024 or 42, meaning that 42 patients with MI must be treated with aspirin to prevent one death. If a drug or procedure is associated with an adverse outcome, then a similar calculation can be used to derive the number needed to harm.

Sensitivity, specificity and usefulness of tests

Absolute risk reduction, the risk ratio, OR and NNT (or harm) are appropriate for looking at differences in risk between two groups, both for observational epidemiology and for clinical trials. In clinical practice, it is also necessary to have a statistical measure suitable for the analysis of diagnostic tests.

Sensitivity

The sensitivity of a test is its ability to pick up a condition:

Sensitivity =

Number of true positives detected

All true positives

A test that is 95% sensitive will detect 95% of all cases (or, put another way, miss 5% of cases).

Specificity

The specificity of a test is defined as follows:

Specificity =

Number of true negatives detected

All true negatives

A 75% specificity means that 75% of all true negatives will test negative or, conversely, that 25% of true negatives will test positive.

Usefulness of tests and positive and negative predictive values

Sensitivity and specificity are the absolute properties of a test, but they do not necessarily demonstrate whether a test is useful in clinical practice. This depends just as much on the likelihood that a person has a condition in the first place. If the pretest probability that a patient has a particular condition is very low, then most positive tests will be false positives, even if the test has, in absolute terms, a high specificity.

The practical usefulness of a test in a given population can be summarised using:

- positive predictive value (the chance that a positive will be a true positive in that population);

- negative predictive value (the chance that a negative will be a true negative in that population).

Positive and negative predictive values are really a mathematical demonstration of the common-sense observation that if you ask a silly question you get a silly answer. Figure 3 demontrates this. In both situations the test in question has a sensitivity of 95% and specificity of 95%, which would be reasonable in clinical practice. In Fig. 3a the test is

applied to a population where the prevalence is 1%; in Fig. 3b it is aplied to a population with a prevalence of 10%. In the 1% prevalence scenario the ratio of false to true posives is 5.2:1. In the 10% prevalence scenario, using an identical test, the ratio of false to true positives is around 1:2.

In practical terms this means that, even with a test with a reasonably good specificity, if you perform the test on a patient with a very low probability of disease, there is a high probability that a positive test is a false positive. This is a good reason not to do tests where the patient is unlikely to have the disease: it is more likely to confuse than help the situation. Ticking every test box mindlessly is not just wasteful, it is bad and potentially dangerous medicine.

> Positive and negative predictive values refer only to the population in which a study was done because they depend as much on the prevalence of the condition being tested as on the accuracy of the test.

Power calculations and error types

Power calculations

It is essential that power calculations are performed before a study begins. A study that is underpowered is both pointless and unethical (see Section 3). The best years of many young researchers' lives have been wasted (along with a lot of money) pursuing studies that were clearly underpowered to detect the thing they were looking for.

Physicians do not need to understand the technicalities of power calculations; there are several formulae for different situations and all statistical packages will perform

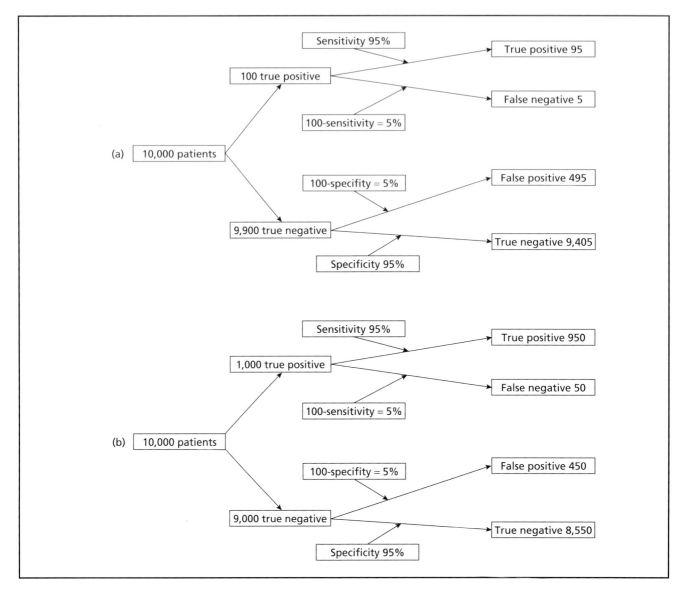

▲ **Fig. 3** (**a**) True- and false-positive and true- and false-negative results generated by a test with a sensitivity of 95% and a specificity of 95% when there is a prevalence of 1% for true disease. (**b**) True- and false-positive and true- and false-negative results generated by a test with a sensitivity of 95% and a specificity of 95% when there is a prevalence of 10% for true disease.

power calculations. However, the physician has to decide on three things for a power calculation to be performed in a study comparing two groups.

1. How common is the condition in the reference population? Generally, the rarer the condition, the larger the study will need to be.

2. How big a difference do you want to detect? The smaller the difference you want to detect, the larger the study will have to be.

3. How strict do you want to be in interpreting the data? There is a conventional default for this, but in certain circumstances you need to be stricter.

An example: let us say that you want to do a trial with expensive new drug A against conventional treatment in meningitis. Assume that the two arms of your study are of equal size.

- If 30% die with conventional treatment and you were only interested in halving mortality

(because smaller effects are not economically justifiable), you would need 266 patients.

- If 30% die currently and you were interested in detecting a 20% reduction in mortality, you would need 1,782 patients.

- If 10% currently die and you wanted to halve it, you would need 948 patients.

- If 10% currently die and you wanted to detect a 20% reduction, you would need 6,624 patients.

It is important to remember that power calculations are a minimum number.

Error types

Studies that are underpowered have the chance to fall into one of two major statistical errors: type 1 or type 2.

Type 1 error Formally, a type 1 error is where the null hypothesis is falsely rejected. In practice, this means that the study claims to find a difference that does not really exist, ie the result is just a statistical fluke.

The conventional cut-off for significance is P of 0.05, or a 1 in 20 chance. In theory, therefore, if 20 random small studies were conducted, you would expect to get one that was 'positive' by chance alone. The bigger the study, the less chance there is that this will happen. This is covered more fully in Section 3.

Type 2 error Formally, a type 2 error is where the null hypothesis is falsely accepted. This means that a researcher claims that there is no difference between two groups, when in reality the trial was just too small to detect a difference. This is exceptionally common, even in papers published in the leading journals. For a study to be capable of excluding a difference between one group and another, you usually need very large numbers (several thousands). Unfortunately, authors often feel that a paper claiming to show that 'drug A is as good as drug B' will be published, whereas one (however large and well conducted) that simply states 'we were unable to detect a difference between drug A and drug B, but the study was only capable of detecting a 20% difference' will not. Regrettably they are probably right; editors and readers like positive results.

FURTHER READING

Bland M. *An Introduction to Medical Statistics*, 3rd edn. Oxford: Oxford University Press, 2000.

Kirkwood BR and Sterne JAC. *Essentials of Medical Statistics*, 2nd edn. Oxford: Blackwell Science, 2003.

Basic concepts

To understand clinical studies in the general medical press, it is essential to have a working knowledge of basic epidemiological methods because most clinical studies and all clinical trials use these methods in both study design and analysis. There are only five basic classes of study design, although there are several variations on each theme, and it is important to decide which one a researcher is using:

- cross-sectional studies;
- comparative (or geographical/ecological) studies;
- case–control studies;
- cohort studies;
- randomised clinical trials (dealt with in detail in Section 3), which are a variation on cohort studies.

Each has advantages and limitations. To understand the pros and cons, it is helpful to remember a few simple concepts.

Exposure, outcome and association

> All studies are looking at an exposure, and seeing whether it is associated with an outcome. This may involve:
>
> - watching (an observational study);
> - doing something (an intervention study).
>
> The exposure might be a drug and the outcome a stroke (in a clinical trial), or the exposure might be radiation and the outcome cancer (an observational study). It must always be clear from the study design what exposure, or exposures, the study is investigating.

Epidemiology identifies associations between exposure and disease, but finding an association does not necessarily establish causality. There is, for example, an extremely strong association between having black skin and childhood malaria, yet nobody is going to claim that black skin causes malaria – it is just that most of those exposed to malaria are African. Associations have to be interpreted with caution and common sense, but if a very strong association is demonstrated (eg between lung cancer and smoking) and it makes biological sense, it is usually reasonable to assume that the exposure is a risk factor for the disease.

Prevalence and incidence

> - Prevalence is the frequency of a condition in the community at a given point in time (eg 23% of the population aged over 85 years have osteoarthritis).
> - Incidence is the frequency of a disease occurring over a period in time (eg 1 in 1,000 children had measles in the year 2000).

Prevalence is mainly useful for describing chronic conditions in which, once a patient has the condition, he or she has it for life. Incidence is almost always the best way to describe acute but short-lived conditions. The importance of this difference should be clear if we compare psoriasis and chickenpox.

- Chickenpox is a very common disease in the sense that almost everybody in the UK will have it once, but it is short-lived. At any given time, the prevalence of chickenpox is very low, but the incidence among children will be high.

- Psoriasis, on the other hand, is relatively much less common, but remains important for the rest of a patient's life. The number of new cases diagnosed in any given year is relatively small so the incidence is small, yet the prevalence is relatively high and gives a far better indication of how great a burden of disease there is in the community.

Sometimes it is obvious that it is best to use prevalence, sometimes incidence and sometimes both have advantages. If you want to study stroke prevention you will be interested in changes in stroke incidence, because it is the rate of new strokes that is important. If you are trying to plan the number of beds a health authority will need for stroke patients, the prevalence of those who have suffered a severe stroke will be more helpful.

Confounding

The last important concept is confounding, and this is the only thing in epidemiology that is not just applied common sense.

Confounding is a distortion where one exposure is associated with another exposure that is also a risk factor for a disease. This can cause incorrect conclusions to be drawn. It is important to remember that, to be a confounding factor, something must be associated both with exposure and with the outcome. This can be expressed diagrammatically (Fig. 4).

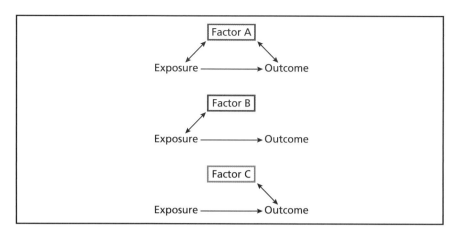

▲ **Fig. 4** Relationships between factors that do and do not confound a study. Only factor A is a confounding factor.

It is easiest to understand confounding by considering an extreme example. If we are interested in risk factors for a disease, we might take a work sample where some of the employees enjoy themselves drinking at the pub of an evening whereas another group go to the fitness club. We might ask the question: how protective is exercise for heart disease? If we look at the fitness enthusiasts, we would probably find that they have much less heart disease and it would be tempting to claim that exercise is highly protective against heart disease – tempting but probably wrong. Those who go to the pub and those who go to the gym are likely to have a whole raft of different behaviours that are associated both with their pastimes and with heart disease. It is likely that the keep-fit enthusiasts will

also eat lower-fat foods, drink less alcohol, smoke less and come from different socioeconomic backgrounds to those who go to the pub. On the other hand, there may be some people who started to go to the gym because they have heart disease. All these will confuse the issue, because they are associated with both the exposure (exercise) and the outcome (heart disease), as seen with factor A in Fig. 4.

The art of epidemiology is to think about what might be confounding factors when you ask a question, which requires both imagination and general medical knowledge; and then to design studies that get around them, control for them or minimise them as much as possible.

2.1 Observational studies

Types of study

To identify associations and minimise confounding, four main epidemiological techniques have been designed. Each has strengths and weaknesses (summarised in Table 3). They are:

1. geographical (ecological) studies;
2. cross-sectional (prevalence) studies;
3. case–control studies;
4. cohort studies.

TABLE 3 STRENGTHS (+) AND WEAKNESSES (−) OF DIFFERENT OBSERVATIONAL STUDY DESIGNS AND OF RANDOMISED TRIALS

	Geographical	Cross-sectional	Case–control	Cohort	Randomised trial
Rare disease	++++	−	+++++	−	−
Rare exposure	++	−	−	+++++	+++++
Multiple outcomes	+	++	−	+++++	+++++
Multiple exposures	++	++	++++	+	+
Time relationships (incidence)	−	−	+	+++++	+++++
Eliminates bias	−	−	−	−	++++

Geographical (ecological) studies

Geographical studies are excellent at generating hypotheses, although less helpful at testing them. At their most basic, a physician sits in a library and notices from published data that, for instance, there is far more bowel cancer in Britain than in Kenya. There are many possible reasons for this (genetic, sunlight, dietary – you think them up!). Some of these can be excluded because they are clearly nonsense, but this still leaves many possible exposures that could give rise to the disease. The genetic possibilities are most easily tested by looking at migrants. What happens to ethnic Kenyans who live a Western lifestyle in Britain? If they take on the risk of a white resident, the risk factor is probably environmental; if they (and their children) keep the Kenyan risk, it is probably genetic. It may be both.

Medically important hypotheses that have been raised by geographical studies include some of the earlier evidence that hypertension plays a part in cardiovascular disease, that salt promotes hypertension and that high-fibre diets are protective against colon cancer. Studies may sometimes simply use existing data to generate hypotheses.

Example 1: Geographical study

Figure 5 shows the correlation between the incidence of colon cancer in women and daily meat consumption per head of population in 23 countries.

The methodology used in geographical studies is very fast because the data are already gathered and in the public domain, but:

- it does not allow examination of any confounding factors;
- 'routine' data (eg death certificates) are often inaccurate.

An alternative is to do a survey in two areas. This is slower, but:

- data will be gathered in a standardised way;
- information on confounding factors can be examined.

Example 2: Geographical study

A study of dental caries in children in six locations in the USA showed that the prevalence of teeth free of dental caries varied from 11 to 56%. All the worst three towns had a fluoride content in their local water sources of less than 1.6 ppm; all the best three had local fluoride contents of 1.7–2.5 ppm. This raised the possibility that fluoride in water protects against caries. This was subsequently proved by an intervention study.

The main difficulty with geographical studies is that differences between two areas that cannot be controlled for cannot be excluded, nor can those that have not even been considered. Hypotheses generated by geographical studies therefore almost always need to be tested subsequently by other means.

Cross-sectional (prevalence) studies

Cross-sectional studies look at the number of cases of a disease at a particular point in time. The main advantage of cross-sectional studies is that they are excellent for estimating prevalence of a disease and the methodology is simple. The main technical difficulty is ensuring a representative sample.

Example 3: Cross-sectional study

A sample of people aged 75 or over living in Cambridge in 1968 had a Mini-Mental State Examination; if they scored less than 26 points, they were examined by a psychiatrist in a standardised way. The study demonstrated a 10% overall prevalence of dementia, with rates doubling every 5 years.

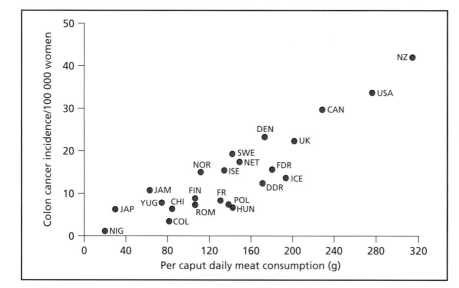

▲ **Fig. 5** Correlation between the incidence of colon cancer in women and per caput daily meat consumption.

As cross-sectional studies are the best method of measuring prevalence of a condition, they are often used in public health for planning purposes. Cross-sectional studies can look at multiple possible outcomes (eg the same study could look for dementia, rheumatoid arthritis and diabetes) because the main problem with them is assembling the representative sample; once this is done, additional tests add little to the work.

In principle, cross-sectional studies can also look at multiple exposures. However, they are usually not good for testing hypotheses about the relationship between exposure and outcome in detail, because it is difficult to deal with potential confounding factors in a structured way. In addition, they are not useful for investigating either rare diseases or rare exposures (a cross-sectional survey will not identify many, or any, examples) and they can look only at prevalence, not incidence, of diseases.

To get around these problems, two methods have been developed which are the backbone of almost all observational epidemiology: case–control studies and cohort studies.

Case–control studies

In essence, case–control studies are simple. A researcher identifies cases of a disease and then selects a group of control individuals who do not have the disease but who are close to the patients who do in every other way. The researcher then compares the exposures of interest between the cases and the controls. If the cases have higher levels of an exposure, it may be a risk factor for a disease. If the controls have a higher level of an exposure, it may be protective.

Example 4: Case–control study

Use of the oestrogen pill in 94 patients with endometrial carcinoma and 188 controls was compared. Of those with endometrial carcinoma, 57% took the pill compared with 15% of the controls. This raised the possibility that conjugated oestrogen may be a risk factor for endometrial cancer.

However, case–control studies have a number of major pitfalls and can be done very badly indeed. The reasons almost always revolve around the selection of the controls. If the controls are badly selected, it may fatally bias the study. This is best seen with an example. Let us say that we wanted to study alcohol as a potential risk factor for breast cancer. We select our cases from the breast clinic, and take an alcohol history. Who can be the controls? The easiest thing is to select another group from within the hospital – orthopaedic wards are a favourite. The problem with this is that alcohol is a major risk factor for fracture, so the patients do not provide a good comparison. Similarly, those attending antenatal clinics (another traditional comparison for studies in women) are a bad comparison because pregnant women almost always cut down on alcohol. The chest clinic will usually contain smokers, and there is a strong correlation between alcohol use and smoking in many cultures. The gastroenterology wards are even worse. And so on.

There is nothing particularly clever about spotting these potential problems; it simply requires imagination, common sense and general medical knowledge. It is therefore surprising how many very poor control groups are published in the literature. There is no such thing as an ideal control group, but some

are significantly worse than others. Generally the ideal is a community-based study, where the control lives in the same area as the case, but getting controls from the community is notoriously difficult and expensive.

With this caution, case–control studies are excellent in many situations and are the most widely used technique in observational epidemiology.

In general, the advantages are that:

- they are quick and relatively cheap (you do it over a limited time period);
- it is possible to measure multiple exposures;
- you can try to measure all potential confounding factors that you can think of;
- they are excellent with rare diseases (because you start with the cases, they can generally be as rare as you like, eg the amyloid clinic providing amyloid cases).

The disadvantages include the following.

- Difficulty in selecting appropriate controls.
- Case–control studies are not good at looking at a rare exposure. Beryllium may be a serious risk for a stomach ulcer, but as exposure to beryllium is so rare a case–control study comparing beryllium exposure in those with and those without an ulcer will probably not find it in either. This only ceases to be the case when the relationship between exposure and disease is so strong that almost all cases will have exposure (eg mesothelioma with asbestos).

Cohort studies

In cohort studies, one group with an exposure of interest and another without that exposure are selected. Both are then watched over time to see whether the group with the exposure develops the outcomes of interest more or less frequently. Clinical trials, which are discussed in much greater detail below, are a form of cohort study in which the researcher has set the exposure (eg drug or placebo).

 Example 5: Cohort study

In 1951, 40,637 British doctors replied to a questionnaire about their smoking habits, and on the basis of this were classified as either smokers or non-smokers. They were sent subsequent questionnaires over a 10-year period to see if they were still smoking. All deaths and death register causes of death were notified to the study team by the office of the Registrar General. Death from lung cancer was linearly related to the amount smoked. Moreover, it was found that this increased risk dropped steadily after smokers gave up smoking, so that by about 15 years after giving up the excess risk had almost disappeared. This not only confirmed that smoking was detrimental, but also that giving up smoking was beneficial. Data on the relationship of smoking to many other fatal diseases were also provided.

Cohort studies have the same problem as case–control studies in trying to select two groups that do not automatically bias the result. Trials generally get around bias by randomisation (see Section 3), but observational studies cannot. Take an example: is cotton dust a risk factor for asthma? The most obvious thing might be to compare workers in a cotton factory with a matched group from the same area. Unfortunately, this almost automatically biases the study, because employed workers are almost invariably healthier than the population as a whole for a variety of reasons, including pre-appointment health screening and

the fact that the person with serious asthma may not be working at all (termed the 'healthy worker effect').

The advantages of cohort studies are very considerable.

- You can usually define the exposure very closely.

- Multiple possible outcomes can be measured.

- They provide information not just on outcome but on rate of outcome.

- Confounding factors can be measured in great detail prospectively, and do not generally suffer from the danger of recall bias.

- They are particularly useful for looking at a rare exposure as a risk for common diseases, because the researcher predefines the exposure.

The disadvantages of cohort studies are technical and practical.

- The main technical limitation is that they are not good for studying rare diseases or even moderately uncommon ones. You could study 700 men split into two exposure groups for 30 years but would be unlikely to get a single case of hypopituitarism, or even hypothyroidism, in that time. Measuring differences of rates of these conditions in the two groups would therefore be meaningless, 0:0 being the likely outcome.

- The other main problem with cohort studies is that they take a long time and are therefore very expensive. There is often a high dropout rate. In addition there is the very real possibility that, by the time you have finished the study, the burning question you set out to answer has been answered by other means, or that new techniques or definitions have rendered your initial question irrelevant or meaningless.

Nevertheless, observational cohort studies have provided many of the most robust insights in epidemiology.

Dealing with potential bias and confounding

Bias

Bias in a study is a flaw in design that leads to a built-in likelihood that the wrong result will (or may) be obtained. It cannot be controlled for or adjusted at the analysis stage.

The various examples given above show examples of where bias may occur. If you read a paper that has clear, or potential, bias in the way that the study is designed, it has to be considered uninterpretable. It might as well not have been done. In fact, in so far as it is misleading, it is better that it had not been done: it is not only a great waste of time and money, but may also lead to dangerous mistakes. It cannot be stressed enough that bias is not a matter of faulty analysis but almost always of poor initial study design – a failure of common sense at the beginning of a study rather than of mathematics at the end.

Confounding

Confounding has to be taken into account in study design, but it is possible to make some adjustment for it at the analysis stage. There are two broad ways of dealing with confounding:

- restriction;
- stratification.

These seldom eliminate confounding, but do reduce it.

An example: we might be interested in the extent to which smoking is a risk factor for heart disease among healthcare workers. We know that men are at higher risk of heart disease than women. We also know that men smoke more than women. In addition there are several other factors that might well confound one another, including alcohol, stress, exercise, family history and socioeconomic background. We cannot eliminate these complex interactions, so we must try to take them into account.

Restriction One way to deal with this problem is to try to restrict the analysis to people who are as similar as possible, eg compare the smoking male doctors with the non-smoking male doctors, rather than considering all male healthcare workers. This will remove a certain amount of the confounding, although not all. However, it will also make the results much less applicable, because they will say nothing about all other healthcare workers or women.

Stratification An alternative is to stratify. We compare heart disease in women who are smokers with that in women who are non-smokers, and obtain a chi-squared (χ^2) statistic for them. We repeat it for the smoking and non-smoking men, and get another χ^2 statistic for them. We then combine the two χ^2 values, weighted by the relative number of men and women in the study. This largely eliminates confounding by sex, because men are only compared with men and women with women. This method, called Mantel–Haenszel stratification, is a variation on the ordinary χ^2 test.

It is possible to stratify by several different confounding factors simultaneously, using more advanced statistical methods. The most commonly used is logistic regression. Provided that a study is large enough, this can control for many different factors simultaneously. So, for example, young female teetotal smokers are compared only with young female teetotallers who do not smoke, while simultaneously the male teetotallers and the male drinkers are only compared with themselves, and a grand summary statistic is calculated for all of them together.

Mantel–Haenszel stratification can be done with a hand calculator; logistic regression can be done only by a computer, but for the operator it is equally easy because the computer takes the strain. Understanding how it is done is not necessary: physicians only have to understand that stratification can be done and that it is relatively easy, provided that potential confounding factors have been thought of and recorded for all cases in the first place.

FURTHER READING

Dean HT. Endemic fluorosis and its relation to dental caries. *Public Health Rep.* 1938; 53: 1443–52.

Doll R and Bradford Hill A. Mortality in relation to smoking: ten years' observation of British doctors. *BMJ* 1964; 1: 1399–410; 1460–7.

O'Connor DW, Politt PA, Hyde JB, *et al.* The prevalence of dementia as measured by the Cambridge Mental Disorders of the Elderly Examination. *Acta Psychiatr. Scand.* 1989; 79: 190–8.

Zeil HK and Finkle WD. Increased risk of endometrial carcinoma among users of conjugated estrogens. *N. Engl. J. Med.* 1975; 293: 1167–70.

Clinical trials are medical experiments. They are used to evaluate the potential benefits and the potential hazards of various medical 'interventions', including medicines, surgical procedures, diagnostic tests, management strategies and aspects of health policy. Meta-analyses of randomised trials are syntheses of studies about similar questions.

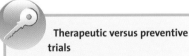

Therapeutic versus preventive trials

- Therapeutic trials: these trials involve patients with an existing disease. They try to determine the ability of an intervention to reduce symptoms, prevent recurrence or decrease the risk of death from that disease. For example, can *Helicobacter pylori* eradication regimens relieve symptoms in infected patients with non-ulcer dyspepsia?
- Preventive trials: these trials involve evaluation of whether an agent or procedure reduces the risk of developing disease among those free from that condition at enrolment. For example, can strategies of mass *Helicobacter pylori* eradication in the general population reduce the eventual incidence of gastric cancer?

The practice of medicine is increasingly based on clinical trials and meta-analyses of clinical trials, so physicians should be able to understand general issues related to their design, analysis and interpretation. The main focus of this section is on trials and meta-analyses with major clinical outcomes, such as death and serious morbidity.

Features of clinical trials with reliable methods

Design:

- Proper randomisation.
- Large number of events (deaths or serious clearly defined morbidity).
- Appropriate 'control' intervention (such as placebo tablets, standard treatment or different dosages of the same intervention).

Analysis:

- Analysis by allocated treatments (ie 'intention-to-treat' analysis).
- Emphasis on the overall results (subgroup analyses can be misleading).

Interpretation:

- Systematic meta-analysis of all the relevant randomised trials (emphasis on the results of one or another particular study can be misleading).

Large-scale randomised evidence

- Large treatment effects can usually be spotted in observational studies and in small trials.
- Modest improvements in survival and in serious morbidity (eg reductions in the incidence of stroke or acute myocardial infarction) can still be medically important.
- Large-scale randomised evidence is needed to confirm or exclude moderate effects.

Treatments with spectacular and unequivocal effects on death and major morbidity (such as therapies for malignant hypertension and diabetic ketoacidosis) generally do not require assessment in large clinical trials. Such effects can usually be spotted in observational studies (see Section 2.1) and in small trials, eg the benefits of *Helicobacter pylori* eradication in peptic ulceration are so striking that only a handful of small trials was needed to demonstrate them reliably (Table 4).

Large trials are needed to distinguish between treatments that are 'only' moderately effective and those that are ineffective. How small is a treatment benefit (or hazard) before it is worth knowing about? Reliable knowledge about changes in disease rates of even a few per cent can often be important. Applied to large groups of people, modest benefits from widely practicable treatments for common causes of premature death or serious disability can make big medical differences.

Demonstration of an important effect

Consider aspirin: the ability of daily medium-dose aspirin (75–325 mg) to prevent recurrences in a wide range of people with a previous history of myocardial infarction (MI) or occlusive stroke was reliably demonstrated by a meta-analysis of many randomised trials. Overall, about 9.5% (4,835/51,144) of such patients allocated aspirin for a mean

TABLE 4 RANDOMISED TRIALS OF *HELICOBACTER PYLORI* ERADICATION STRATEGIES IN PEPTIC ULCERATION WITH ABOUT 1-YEAR FOLLOW-UP

Abbreviated reference	Regimen/duration	No. of relapses[1]/total	
		Antibiotic arm	Control arm
Hentschel, *N. Engl. J. Med.* 1993; 328: 308	RMA/2 weeks	4/50 (8%)	42/49 (86%)
Graham, *Ann. Intern. Med.* 1992; 116: 705	RBMT/2 weeks	6/47 (13%)	34/36 (94%)
Marshall, *Lancet* 1988; ii: 1437	BTi/8 weeks	5/20 (25%)	38/50 (76%)
Rauws, *Lancet* 1990; 335: 1233	BMA/4 weeks	3/24 (13%)	16/26 (62%)
Sung, *N. Engl. J. Med.* 1995; 332: 139	BMT/1 week	1/22 (5%)	12/23 (52%)
Graham, *Ann. Intern. Med.* 1992; 116: 705	RBMT/2 weeks	2/15 (7%)	8/11 (73%)
Total		21/178 (12%)	150/195 (77%)

1. Refers to endoscopic ulcer recurrences.
A, amoxicillin; B, bismuth; M, metronidazole; R, ranitidine; T, tetracycline; Ti, tinidazole.

duration of about 2 years died or had a vascular event compared with 11.9% (6,108/51,315) who were allocated control (Table 5). Worldwide, there are more than 10 million deaths each year from MI and stroke, plus a comparable number of disabling non-fatal episodes. As aspirin is cheap, practicable and widely available, appropriately widespread use of it for the treatment and secondary prevention of vascular disease could well avoid more than 100,000 premature deaths annually.

Demonstration of no effect

Just as large-scale randomised evidence can demonstrate modest but important benefits that are overlooked in other trials, it can also refute claims of benefits made in smaller studies.

For example, infusion of magnesium salt in the treatment of acute MI was thought to reduce deaths by about one-quarter. However, this practice was based on studies involving only a few hundred deaths. The ISIS-4

TABLE 5 SUMMARY OF THE OVERALL RESULTS OF TRIALS OF ASPIRIN (OR OTHER ANTIPLATELET DRUGS)[1] FOR THE PREVENTION OF VASCULAR EVENTS: THE ANTIPLATELET TRIALISTS' COLLABORATION (1994), INVOLVING A TOTAL OF ABOUT 100,000 RANDOMISED PATIENTS IN OVER 100 TRIALS

Type of patient	Average scheduled treatment duration (approximate number of patients randomised)	Proportion who suffered a non-fatal stroke, non-fatal heart attack or vascular death during trials		
		Antiplatelet (%)	Control (%)	Events avoided in these trials (per 1,000)
High risk				
Suspected acute heart attack	1 month (20,000)	10	14	40 ($2P<0.00001$)
Previous history of heart attack	2 years (20,000)	13	17	40 ($2P<0.00001$)
Previous history of stroke or transient ischaemic attack	3 years (10,000)	18	22	40 ($2P<0.00001$)
Other vascular disease[2]	1 year (20,000)	7	9	20 ($2P<0.00001$)
Low risk				
Primary prevention in low-risk people	5 years (30,000)	4.4	4.8	4 ($2P>0.05$)

1. The most widely tested regimen was medium-dose aspirin, involving a daily dose of 75–325 mg; no other antiplatelet regimen appeared significantly more or less effective than this in preventing such vascular events.
2. For example, angina, peripheral vascular disease, arterial surgery and angioplasty.

randomised trial, by contrast, involved 58,050 patients with acute MI. About 7.6% (2,216/29,011) of those allocated magnesium died within 1 month copared with 7.2% (2,103/29,039) who were allocated control. This unpromising result suggested that the effect of magnesium had been overestimated by the small earlier studies.

> Reliable information generally comes from large randomised trials (and meta-analyses of such trials) that are interpreted cautiously.

Design of trials

Randomisation

> • Proper randomisation should ensure unbiased comparison.
> • Randomisation is the only method of allocation that achieves control of both known and unknown confounding factors.

> ⚠ Non-random methods involve biases that can mimic or obscure real treatment effects.

Why should patients be allocated at random to different treatment strategies in clinical trials? The answer is simply because other methods are prone to confounding (see Section 2). Non-random methods (eg letting patients or doctors determine treatment allocation) are prone to biased assessments because the characteristics of patients who are allocated different treatments may differ in ways that could influence the results.

> 🔑 **Methods of treatment allocation**
>
> Proper randomisation, which should avoid bias, can be achieved via:
>
> • computer-generated randomisation;
> • random number tables.

> ⚠ **Methods of treatment allocation**
>
> Types of randomisation that are not proper and which are prone to bias include:
>
> • assignment by odd/even number in the patient identification number, by date of birth or by date of presentation;
> • the patient or doctor chooses the treatment;
> • 'historical controls' (comparison with patients treated in the past).

Randomisation ensures that each type of patient (eg young/old, male/female or low risk/high risk) should on average be allocated in similar proportions to the different treatment strategies.

The larger the trial, the more likely that randomisation will produce perfectly balanced groups. This applies not only to patient characteristics that are measured routinely (eg age and severity of disease) but also to those potential confounders that may affect prognosis but which may not be measured. Randomisation is the only method of allocation that achieves control for both known and unknown confounding factors.

In a properly randomised trial, the decision to enter a patient is made irreversibly in ignorance of which trial treatment(s) that patient will be allocated. Otherwise, foreknowledge of the next treatment allocation could affect the decision to enrol

the patient, and those allocated one treatment might then differ in a systematic way from those allocated another. For example, if doctors determined treatment allocations in a clinical trial, people with more severe disease might preferentially receive the treatment believed to be more promising. As patients with more severe disease would be expected to have poorer outcomes than people with less severe disease, this method of allocation might obscure any treatment benefit.

Sample size

> 🔑 • The sample size required for a trial depends on the number of clinical events (eg deaths and relapses) recorded after recruitment.
> • Without a few thousand events for analysis, moderate benefits or hazards of treatment on major outcomes can easily be missed.
> • A common strategy to increase sample size is multicentre participation.
> • A common strategy to increase the proportion of trial participants having clinical events is to study 'high-risk' groups.

The sensitivity of a trial depends not so much on the total number of people recruited into it but on the number of patients who die or suffer relevant clinical events before the statistical analysis takes place. Treatment differences can be detected in trials with varying numbers of relevant events. In general, to test at least a 20% reduction in the primary outcome (such as death or recurrence of a cancer) reliably, a few thousand events are needed for analysis. Obviously, far more patients must be randomised to observe this number.

For example, the 1-month survival advantage produced by aspirin was clearly demonstrated in the ISIS-2 randomised trial of the treatment of acute MI. About 9.4% (804/8,587) of the patients allocated aspirin died from vascular disease compared with 11.8% (1,016/8,600) allocated to placebo control (Fig. 6). Nowadays, aspirin is routinely used in the emergency treatment of MI. Yet, if the ISIS-2 trial had been 10 times smaller (but still large in comparison with other cardiology trials at that time), it would not have been sufficiently sensitive because 80 deaths in the aspirin group versus 100 in the placebo group would not have yielded a statistically significant result. Modest but important benefits (or hazards) cannot be confirmed or ruled out unless properly randomised trials have recorded sizeable numbers of events.

An obvious way of increasing the relevant size of a trial is to increase the recruitment. This can be enhanced by:

- collaboration (eg involvement of clinicians in many different hospitals);

- simplification of the study protocol (eg streamlining enrolment and follow-up procedures).

The ISIS-4 trial, for example, recruited 58,050 patients in only 20 months with the participation of clinicians in more than 1,200 hospitals in 25 countries. Collaborators were asked to record only essential information and patients were then traced by national mortality statistics. There were 4,319 deaths in these patients.

Other ways of increasing the relevant size of trials include prolonging the duration of any follow-up and selecting high-risk populations to study, such as elderly people or those with previous disease. For example, the HOPE randomised study of ramipril versus placebo recruited people with a previous history of vascular disease or diabetes and monitored them for about 5 years. This strategy yielded 1,477 cardiovascular events, many more events than would have been expected in a briefer study or in a study of the general population. The HOPE study was able to

demonstrate reliably that ramipril reduces death and vascular recurrences by about one-fifth. A later section of this module discusses yet another way of increasing the numbers of events available for analysis: meta-analysis of randomised studies.

The study intervention

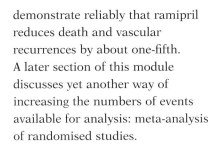

- 'Factorial' studies assess several different treatments in the same trial.
- 'Controlled' trials compare some intervention with a placebo, standard therapy or different dosages of the same treatment.

Poor treatment compliance by patients can mask real benefits.

'Factorial' trials Most trials evaluate just one treatment, but this does not have to be so. 'Factorial' trials test two or more treatments simultaneously. Such comparisons can add to the scientific value and the practical efficiency of a trial ('two answers for the price of one').

For example, the ISIS-2 study was a factorial trial in which a comparison was made between placebo and two drugs (separately and in combination). Patients with suspected MI were randomised to one of four treatments:

1. intravenous streptokinase alone (1,500,000 units over 1 hour);

2. aspirin 160 mg daily alone;

3. both active drugs;

4. double placebo.

This trial not only showed that each of the drugs produced about a 25% reduction in mortality, but that they

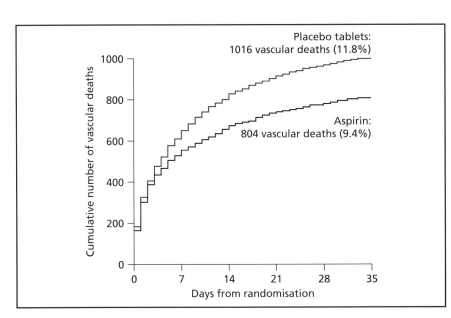

▲ **Fig. 6** Effect of administration of aspirin for 1 month on 35-day vascular mortality in the 1988 ISIS-2 trial, among over 17,000 acute MI patients.

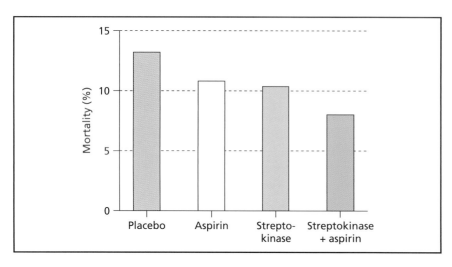

▲ **Fig. 7** Factorial design of ISIS-2. Mortality at 35 days: both streptokinase and aspirin produced a >20% reduction in mortality and the effect of the two therapies was additive.

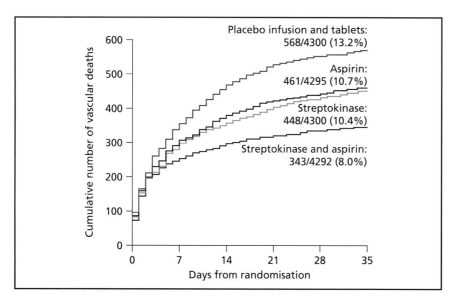

▲ **Fig. 8** Effects of a 1-hour streptokinase infusion (and of 1 month of aspirin) on 35-day vascular mortality in ISIS-2.

were additive in their effects (Figs 7 and 8). The ability to detect any 'interactions' between treatments is another advantage of factorial studies.

'Controlled' trials These are studies in which the effects of a new 'test' treatment are compared with those of an existing therapy, either inactive (placebo) or active. If there is already a treatment of proven value, patients in the control arm should receive it. For example, the IDEAL randomised study compared 80 mg

atorvastatin daily versus 20 mg simvastatin in almost 9,000 patients with a previous history of MI. The trial's control treatment was such because a previous trial had demonstrated that 20 mg simvastatin produced about a 33% reduction in death and recurrences in such patients compared with placebo.

If a standard treatment does not exist, placebo control may help to avoid biases that might arise through knowledge of a patient's treatment status. Indeed in 'double-

blind' studies treatment status is concealed from both patients and doctors. Such measures are particularly necessary when there is a substantial degree of subjectivity, such as the self-reporting of symptoms in trials of non-ulcer dyspepsia and *Helicobacter pylori* eradication.

Compliance There are many reasons why patients fail to take their medications in clinical trials (or in routine clinical practice): they forget, develop side effects, withdraw consent or obtain alternative treatments on their own initiative, etc. Whatever the reasons for it, imperfect compliance has the same effect: it decreases the ability of a trial to detect differences between treatments.

Non-compliance is a particular example of a more general problem in trials, namely ensuring that experimental contrast between treatment and control groups persists for the whole duration of the study. A suboptimal therapy can blunt or obscure real treatment benefits, such as *Helicobacter pylori* eradication regimens with low bacterial 'kill rates'. A treatment with an unsustained action has the same effect, such as reinfection with *Helicobacter pylori* after successful eradication.

Overlap between treatment groups is particularly likely in studies of behavioural interventions. For example, in the MRFIT randomised study 12,866 men at high risk of coronary heart disease received either a special programme to reduce coronary risk factors (such as smoking, BP and blood cholesterol) or usual care. By the end of the study, risk factors in the two groups were more similar than anticipated, partly because some men allocated special treatment did not comply with it, and partly because men allocated usual care adopted healthier habits by the end of the study. Perhaps as a consequence, the study did not demonstrate conclusive benefits for cardiac mortality.

Analysis of trials

Stopping a trial prematurely

Trials stopped prematurely are prone to exaggeration.

A trial may be stopped before its scheduled duration if clear evidence of a benefit or a hazard emerges in the interim. A data monitoring committee, independent of the study investigators, usually monitors interim results. The goal is to protect the interests of the participants in the study as well as the larger population of future potential patients. This can be a tricky balance to strike. For example, a randomised study compared extracorporeal membrane oxygenation with standard medical treatment in newborns with persistent pulmonary hypertension. It was stopped prematurely when four of the ten infants allocated standard treatment died, compared with none of the nine allocated the newer extracorporeal membrane oxygenation. These numbers were small, and many clinicians considered the results unconvincing and so did not accept the newer treatment. A much larger trial, reported several years after the original study, provided much more reliable evidence of benefit, and this evidence persuaded many more clinicians to adopt extracorporeal membrane oxygenation treatment. During this period of uncertainty, the lack of convincing evidence may

well have led to fewer newborns worldwide receiving the new treatment than would have been the case had the original trial continued longer.

Scepticism about interim findings is usually justified.

Experience has shown that emerging trends based on small numbers might well be transient and disappear, or even reverse, after data have accumulated from a larger sample. For example, three separate interim analyses during the first 30 months of the Coronary Drug Project randomised study suggested fewer deaths in those allocated clofibrate than in those allocated placebo ($P < 0.05$). However, the data monitoring committee appropriately regarded this evidence as too weak to warrant stopping the trial early. When the final results were analysed 3 years later, deaths in the clofibrate group were nearly identical to those of the placebo group (25.5% vs 25.4%).

'Intention-to-treat' analysis

The main comparison in a trial should be an 'intention-to-treat' analysis, ie comparison of outcomes among all those originally allocated one treatment with all those allocated the other treatment.

It is easy to spoil the benefits of random allocation by inappropriate analysis of data. A common but mistaken practice is to exclude randomised patients from the main analysis, usually because they were either non-compliant with the study treatment or lost to follow-up. This approach can distort results if the prognosis of those excluded from one treatment group differs from

the prognosis of those excluded from the other group.

Such confounding was demonstrated by the investigators in the Coronary Drug Project trial. Patients who took at least 80% of their allocated clofibrate had substantially lower 5-year mortality rates than those who did not (15.0% vs 24.6%, respectively), but there was an even larger difference in mortality between good and poor compliers in the placebo group (15.1% vs 28.3%, respectively).

The main statistical analysis in any trial should compare outcome among all patients originally allocated one treatment (even though some of them may not have actually received it) with outcome among all those allocated the other treatment. Nowadays, leading medical journals require the reporting of such 'intention-to-treat' analyses for randomised trials, but this does not guarantee that they are actually done. For example, four randomised trials of *Helicobacter pylori* eradication in non-ulcer dyspepsia, all published in leading journals between 1998 and 2000, stated policies of intention-to-treat analyses. However, each excluded certain randomised patients, representing 6% of the total randomised in the four trials combined.

Exploratory analyses and subgroups

Trust an overall result of a study much more than subdivisions of data.

Subgroup analyses can be seriously misleading.

TABLE 6 EXAMPLE OF A MISLEADING SUBGROUP ANALYSIS: FALSE-NEGATIVE MORTALITY EFFECT IN A SUBGROUP DEFINED ONLY BY ASTROLOGICAL BIRTH SIGN: THE ISIS-2 (1988) TRIAL OF ASPIRIN AMONG OVER 17,000 ACUTE MI PATIENTS

Astrological birth sign	Number of 1-month deaths (aspirin vs placebo)	Statistical significance
Libra or Gemini	150 vs 147	NS
All other signs	654 vs 869	$2P < 0.000001$
Any birth sign[1]	804 (9.4%) vs 1,016 (11.8%)	$2P < 0.000001$

1. Appropriate overall analysis for assessing the true effect in all subgroups.

A subgroup analysis refers to subdivision of the main comparison in a study. As patients can be grouped by many different characteristics (age, sex, severity of disease, etc.) and by many combinations of characteristics (eg young men with severe disease or old women with mild disease), exploratory analyses of subgroups can be numerous. This is a problem because each additional statistical comparison increases the risk of a false-positive result, particularly when sparse data are finely divided. Subgroup analyses can either produce spurious results ('torture the data enough, and eventually it will confess') or overlook real differences between subgroups. Only some very large studies (or certain large meta-analyses; see later) have adequate precision to make reliable comparisons about possible treatment differences in subgroups of patients, but even in these very large trials extreme caution is needed to interpret the results appropriately.

Subgroups and lunacy

Consider the classic example provided by the investigators of the ISIS-2 randomised trial of aspirin in acute MI. They demonstrated the unreliability of subgroup analyses by subdividing the clear overall result (804 vascular deaths in the aspirin group versus 1,016 vascular deaths in the placebo group, $P < 0.000001$) by astrological 'birth signs'. Twelve absurd subgroups emerged. In some birth signs, the results for aspirin were about average and in some they were, just by chance, a bit better or a bit worse than average. Libra and Gemini were subgroups with the least promising results: for these two birth signs exclusively, no fewer deaths occurred with aspirin than with placebo (Table 6).

It would obviously be unwise to conclude from this analysis that patients with acute MI born under Libra or Gemini are unlikely to benefit from aspirin. Yet subgroup analyses that are no more statistically reliable than these are frequently reported and accepted, with inappropriate effects on clinical practice. For example, the use of aspirin after transient ischaemic attacks was, until recently, approved in the USA for men but not women because of the selective emphasis on small subgroups in particular trials. In retrospect, this was a lethal mistake, resulting in many women being denied a life-saving treatment that produces about the same benefits for women as for men.

Interpretation of trials

The totality of evidence

Keep your feet on the ground

- Before changing your clinical behaviour in response to a particular trial, consider all other relevant randomised studies on that therapeutic question (or, even better, consult a well-conducted meta-analysis).
- Be wary of initial small trials with extreme findings; their apparent promise may be short-lived.

As described later, meta-analysis of all relevant trials on a therapeutic question is one way of reducing false-negative and false-positive results in particular studies. It is especially helpful when new trials report their findings in the context of an updated meta-analysis of previous trials. For example, the placebo-controlled PEP study randomised 13,356 patients undergoing surgery for hip fractures to 160 mg aspirin daily, started preoperatively and continued for 35 days. About 1.6% (105/6,679) of the patients allocated aspirin had pulmonary embolism or deep venous thrombosis compared with 2.5% (165/6,677) allocated placebo. The conclusions of PEP were reinforced by a meta-analysis of all previous relevant trials of aspirin, including data from about 9,000 additional patients who were undergoing orthopaedic or general surgery or at high risk of venous thromboembolism for medical reasons.

What is a reasonable attitude to take when a small trial reports an extreme observation but the total evidence on that therapeutic question is still sparse? In general, be sceptical. Small-scale randomised studies may provide misleading results not just of the size but also of the direction of the effects of treatment on major outcomes. For example, it was concluded from a randomised placebo-controlled trial among 500 patients with heart failure that 60 mg daily of the inotropic agent vesnarinone more than halved the risk of death (33 placebo versus 13 vesnarinone deaths). In contrast, when the same regimen was studied in a much larger number of the same type of patients, mortality in those taking vesnarinone was significantly increased (242 placebo versus 292 vesnarinone deaths).

There are many other examples of extreme observations from initial small trials not being confirmed by much larger randomised studies (see Further reading for additional examples).

Extrapolation

Is the trial relevant to my patient?

- It is usually necessary to apply information from trials to patients outside the trials, possibly with different characteristics from the study participants.
- Appropriate extrapolation varies from situation to situation.

Participants in trials may be a skewed subset of the entire target population, eg participants are, by definition, volunteers who may be more health conscious than non-volunteers. Also, some trials involve only specific groups, such as men, white people, middle-aged people or those who have previously suffered from a disease. How can the findings of such studies be applied to groups outside the trials?

In these situations, it is important to note the distinction between:

- proportional benefits (eg a 40% proportional risk reduction, from 10% to 6%);

- absolute benefits (in the above example, 4% or 40 events avoided per 1,000 treated).

When the proportional effect of treatment on some particular outcome appears to be about constant in different patients in trials, a reasonable policy of extrapolation is to apply the proportional reduction observed in the trials to the absolute risk of the outcome in the particular group outside the trial.

For example, a reduction in diastolic BP of 5–6 mmHg achieved in trials of antihypertensive therapy produced proportional risk reductions of about 40% for stroke and 15% for coronary heart disease. Each of these proportional effects appeared to be similar among a broad range of individuals in Europe and North America. How would these results be applied to people in Russia? The absolute risk of stroke and coronary heart disease is several times higher in Russia than in western European countries. This implies that the absolute benefit of blood pressure lowering for vascular disease should be even greater among Russians than among

Westerners, assuming that the proportional effects are similar in Russia to those in Western populations.

Meta-analysis of trials

Strengths and limitations

A meta-analysis can provide a less biased, more precise and more detailed assessment of the available information on a topic than individual studies can.

- The preferential publication of striking results in small studies ('publication bias') may skew meta-analyses.
- The reliability of a meta-analysis depends on the quality and quantity of the data that go into it.

'Meta-analysis' refers to the practice of combining data. Its aim is to provide a more comprehensive assessment of a topic than individual studies can. However, not all meta-analyses of randomised trials are trustworthy. There are two main concerns.

- How carefully was the overview performed?

- How large is it?

The simplest approach is merely to collect and tabulate the published data from whatever randomised trial reports are easily accessible in the literature. However, this approach will miss relevant trials and the studies included may be unrepresentative as a result of the preferential publication of extremely promising or extremely pessimistic results ('publication bias').

At the opposite extreme, meta-analyses can make extensive efforts to locate every potentially relevant randomised trial in systematic searches of the published and unpublished medical literature, to seek individual data on each patient ever randomised into those trials, to check and correct the original data, and then to produce analyses in collaboration with the original trialists. When they are really large, such meta-analyses may actually provide statistically reliable subgroup analyses of the effect of treatment in particular types of patient.

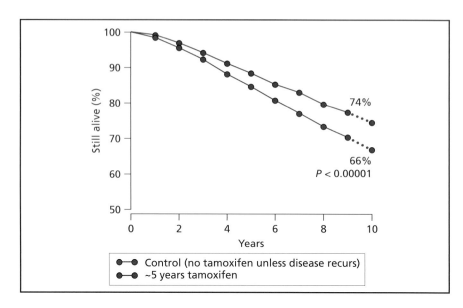

▲ **Fig. 9** Effects of hormonal adjuvant tamoxifen for early breast cancer on 10-year survival in a worldwide overview of randomised trials. The graph shows the survival of all women with potentially hormone-sensitive breast cancer with and without tamoxifen.

The power of a well-conducted meta-analysis

Consider the Early Breast Cancer Trialists' Collaborative Group ('early' breast cancer refers to disease limited to the breast and the locoregional lymph nodes, which can be removed surgically). Taken separately, most of the trials of adjuvant tamoxifen were too small to provide reliable evidence about long-term survival. However, when the original data of 55 trials involving about 37,000 women were combined in 1995, some very definite differences in 10-year survival emerged. For example, among women with potentially hormone-sensitive breast cancer, being treated for about 5 years with adjuvant tamoxifen improved the 10-year survival rate from 66 to 74% (Fig. 9).

Another important aspect of this meta-analysis was that it was large enough to look reliably at tamoxifen's effects in particular subgroups of women. Before this report, tamoxifen was not usually given to younger patients with early breast cancer because most clinicians did not believe that it helped premenopausal women. However, the meta-analysis found that the proportional benefits of tamoxifen were similar in all women irrespective of age, menopausal

status, spread to local lymph nodes or use of chemotherapy. The report concluded that another 20,000 lives each year could be saved worldwide if tamoxifen was given immediately after surgery to all breast cancer patients who needed it, regardless of age and other characteristics.

Interpreting 'forest plots'

Meta-analyses often use diagrams, such as 'forest plots', to summarise large amounts of information.

Meta-analyses should aim to present information concisely and in an accessible way. The use of certain diagrams, sometimes called 'forest plots', can achieve both these aims. There can be minor variations in the form of such plots in the medical literature, but the diagrams typically summarise key information from each of the studies in an overview in only a single row of a table. Plotting the results of individual studies on a common axis provides a convenient

visual comparison of the separate trial results, and a synthesis of the data can be shown graphically on the same plot.

As an example, consider the Antiplatelet Trialists' Collaboration, briefly mentioned at the start of this section. By 1994, this meta-analysis involved information from 145 randomised trials of aspirin or other antiplatelet therapies, mainly related to the secondary prevention of vascular disease. Figure 10 shows just the 11 trials of antiplatelet regimens in patients with prior MI. Note the following.

- A single row in the table summarises information from a particular trial, including the drug regimen, numbers allocated to each treatment and the corresponding numbers of vascular events in each group.

- The horizontal axis of the graph represents the odds of avoiding death or recurrences of MI or stroke on antiplatelet treatment compared with control, an odds ratio (OR) of 1.0 indicating no difference whatsoever.

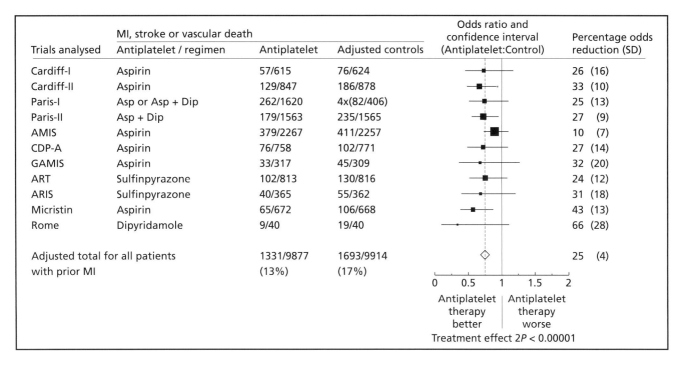

Trials analysed	MI, stroke or vascular death			Odds ratio and confidence interval (Antiplatelet:Control)	Percentage odds reduction (SD)
	Antiplatelet / regimen	Antiplatelet	Adjusted controls		
Cardiff-I	Aspirin	57/615	76/624		26 (16)
Cardiff-II	Aspirin	129/847	186/878		33 (10)
Paris-I	Asp or Asp + Dip	262/1620	4x(82/406)		25 (13)
Paris-II	Asp + Dip	179/1563	235/1565		27 (9)
AMIS	Aspirin	379/2267	411/2257		10 (7)
CDP-A	Aspirin	76/758	102/771		27 (14)
GAMIS	Aspirin	33/317	45/309		32 (20)
ART	Sulfinpyrazone	102/813	130/816		24 (12)
ARIS	Sulfinpyrazone	40/365	55/362		31 (18)
Micristin	Aspirin	65/672	106/668		43 (13)
Rome	Dipyridamole	9/40	19/40		66 (28)
Adjusted total for all patients with prior MI		1331/9877 (13%)	1693/9914 (17%)		25 (4)

Antiplatelet therapy better | Antiplatelet therapy worse

Treatment effect 2P < 0.00001

▲ **Fig. 10** Meta-analysis of 11 randomised trials of prolonged antiplatelet therapy versus control in patients with prior MI. Test for heterogeneity: $\chi^2_{10} = 12.3$; $P > 0.1$; NS. Asp, aspirin; Dip, dipyridamole.

- Black squares represent ORs in each study, with the area of the square proportional to the number of events in each study, eg the AMIS study involves a larger number of vascular events than any of the other trials in Fig. 10, so the area of its square is the largest.

- Horizontal lines emerging from the squares represent confidence intervals (CIs). Larger studies have narrower CIs than smaller studies: once again, as a result of its size, the AMIS study has the narrowest CI of the 11 trials.

- In this example, the overall result and its CI are indicated by an unshaded diamond. Note the diamond's narrow width. This indicates a high degree of precision as a result of the combination of the 11 separate results.

- Overall, the studies indicate a 25% reduction in vascular events among patients allocated antiplatelet treatment compared with those allocated control. The 'test for heterogeneity' indicates that there was no significant statistical scatter among the 11 separate results ($P > 0.1$).

This particular example demonstrates several of the advantages of meta-analysis. Taken separately, 8 of the 11 trials in Fig. 10 were too small to have yielded statistically reliable evidence on their own (as each of their CIs was consistent with an OR of 1.0). Furthermore, in retrospect, the three other trials were significant only because, by chance, they had results that were too good to be true. In contrast, the overall result indicating a 25% reduction in vascular recurrences and death was clear and convincing ($P < 0.00001$).

Ethics in randomised trials

> There must be sufficient doubt about a therapy to withhold it from half the patients in a trial, and at the same time there must be sufficient belief in the therapy's potential to justify giving it to the remaining half.

The Declaration of Helsinki has been accepted internationally as the basis for ethical clinical research. The rights of patients include:

- the liberty to abstain from a study;

- the provision of adequate information about potential benefits and potential hazards of involvement;

- the desirability (a requirement in most cases) of giving written consent before participation;

- the freedom to withdraw from a study at any time.

In the UK, investigators must submit research protocols for review to local research ethics committees or, in the case of multicentre trials, to a regional committee.

When randomised trials recruit patients according to the 'uncertainty principle', there is usually a reasonable parallel between good science and good ethics. This principle states that the fundamental criterion for eligibility is that both patient and doctor should be substantially uncertain about the appropriateness of each of the trial treatments for that particular patient. If there are strong preferences for one or another treatment (by either the patient or the doctor), then that patient is ineligible. However, if both parties are substantially uncertain then randomisation is appropriate.

FURTHER READING

Collins R and MacMahon S. Reliable assessment of the effects of treatment on mortality and major morbidity, I: clinical trials. *Lancet* 2001; 357: 373–80.

- - - - - - - - - - - - - - - - -

Collins R, Peto R, Gray R, *et al*. Large-scale randomised evidence: trials and overviews. In: Warrell DA, Cox TM, Firth JD, *et al*., eds. *Oxford Textbook of Medicine*, 4th edn. Oxford: Oxford University Press, 2003: 24–36.

- - - - - - - - - - - - - - - - -

Hennekens CH and Buring JE. *Epidemiology in Medicine*. Boston: Little, Brown, 1987.

- - - - - - - - - - - - - - - - -

Peto R, Pike MC, Armitage P, *et al*. Design and analysis of randomised clinical trials requiring prolonged observation of each patient (parts I and II). *Br. J. Cancer* 1976; 34: 585–612 (part I); 1977; 35: 1–39 (part II).

- - - - - - - - - - - - - - - - -

Pocock SJ. *Clinical Trials: A Practical Approach*. Chichester: John Wiley & Sons, 1983.

4.1 Self-assessment questions

Question 1

Which one of the following statements is true?

Answers

A The median is the best summary of normally distributed data

B $P < 0.0003$ means that the size of the effect is large

C $P = 0.04$ means a 4% likelihood of obtaining the result by chance alone

D A χ^2 of 12.5 means a 12.5% likelihood of obtaining the result by chance alone

E An odds ratio of 3 corresponds to a three times greater risk for having a disease

Question 2

To test whether drug A reduces mortality more than a placebo, which one of the following statistical tests is most likely to be appropriate?

Answers

A Chi-squared test

B Student's t-test

C Wilcoxon rank-sum test

D Regression analysis

E Mann–Whitney U-test

Question 3

To test for a difference in BP between the populations of London and Edinburgh, which one of the following statistical tests is most likely to be appropriate?

Answers

A Chi-squared test

B Student's t-test

C Wilcoxon rank-sum test

D Regression analysis

E Mann–Whitney U-test

Question 4

To detemine the effect of age on BP, which one of the following statistical tests is most likely to be appropriate?

Answers

A Chi-squared test

B Student's t-test

C Wilcoxon rank-sum test

D Regression analysis

E Mann–Whitney U-test

Question 5

The sensitivity of a test is defined as:

Answers

A Number of true positives detected/all true positives

B Total number of positives detected/all true positives

C Number of true positives detected/number of true negatives detected

D Number of true positives detected/all true negatives

E Total number of positives detected/total number of negatives detected

Question 6

The specificity of a test is defined as:

Answers

A Total number of negatives detected/all true negatives

B Number of true negatives detected/number of false negatives

C Number of true negatives detected/number of true positives detected

D Total number of negatives detected/number of true negatives detected

E Number of true negatives detected/all true negatives

Question 7

A type 1 statistical error occurs when:

Answers

A The null hypothesis is falsely accepted

B The null hypothesis is falsely rejected

C The null hypothesis is inadequately stated

D The null hypothesis does not make biological or clinical sense

E The study is underpowered to answer the question posed

Question 8

Consider a randomised trial of the treatment with aspirin of patients with myocardial infarction. If the probability of death in those given aspirin is $p1$ and the probability of death in those not given aspirin is $p0$, then the number needed to treat to prevent one death is given by:

Answers

A $p0 - p1$

B $p1/p0$

C $p1/(p0 - p1)$

D $1/(p0 - p1)$

E $[p1/(1 - p1)]/[p0/(1 - p0)]$

Question 9

Which one of the following is *not* an advantage of factorial randomised trials?

Answers

A Increased practical efficiency

B The ability to assess directly interactions between two (or more) treatments

C The ability to test more than one intervention

D Additional statistical power

E Additional value for research investment

Question 10

Which one of the following is *not* a potentially biased method to allocate participants to treatments in a trial?

Answers

A Clinical impression

B Coin toss

C Alternation by order of arrival time in the clinic

D Alternation by month of birth (eg odd- versus even-numbered months)

E Degree of likelihood to benefit from a novel treatment

Question 11

Which of the following is most likely to underestimate the true effectiveness of a medication tested in a clinical trial?

Answers

A Frequent interim statistical analyses

B Non-randomised treatment allocation

C Multiple subgroup analyses

D Severe side effects of the treatment

E Placebo control

Question 12

Which of the following statements is true about ethical conduct in randomised trials?

Answers

A Only local research committees can provide ethical oversight

B Doctors should involve their patients in trials even if they are convinced about the benefits of a particular treatment

C Participants should provide a valid reason to withdraw from a study

D Placebo tablets are essential to use in control groups

E Clinical trials without adequate statistical power may be unethical

Question 13

Which one of the following is *not* necessarily a characteristic of optimum trial design?

Answers

A Use of a control arm

B Analysis by intention-to-treat

C Prespecified rules for interim analyses

D Multicentre recruitment

E Collection of biological material

Question 14

Which one of the following factors does *not* influence the statistical power of a clinical trial?

Answers

A Number of participants recruited

B Method of randomisation

C Degree of disease risk of the population being studied

D Duration of follow-up

E Number of interim analyses

Question 15

Which one of the following statements about meta-analyses is *not* true?

Answers

A They involve a combination of data

B They may be distorted by publication bias

C They may enhance statistical power

D They are designed to ignore differences between contributing studies

E They may be based on published data or primary data

Question 16

Which one of the following statements is *not* true of epidemiological 'forest plots'?

Answers

A These diagrams summarise numerical information from trials

B Squares usually represent measures of effect (eg relative risks) and horizontal lines represent confidence intervals

C Smaller studies are represented by smaller squares and wider horizontal lines

D Each study is typically summarised in a row of information

E They provide a visual test for heterogeneity

4.2 Self-assessment answers

Answer to Question 1

C

Normally distributed data should be described by the mean and skewed data by the median. A very small P value means that the result is likely to be statistically significant (has not arisen by chance) but not necessarily that the size of the effect is large: a small effect in a very large study may have a very small P value. Chi-squared values need to be interpreted with tables to derive a probability value. A relative risk of 3 does mean three times the risk, but an odds ratio of 3 corresponds to a smaller risk.

Answer to Question 2

A

Student's *t*-test is used to compare a normally distributed continuous variable between two categorical groups. The Wilcoxon rank-sum test can be used to compare a continuous variable that is not normally distributed between two categorical groups. Regression analysis is used to compare one continuous variable against another continuous variable. The Mann–Whitney *U*-test can be used to compare a continuous variable that is not normally distributed between two categorical groups.

Answer to Question 3

B

The chi-squared test is used to test one categorical variable (drug/placebo) against another categorical variable (dead/alive). For definitions of the Wilcoxon rank-sum test, regression analysis and the Mann–Whitney *U*-test, see answer to Question 2.

Answer to Question 4

D

For definitions of the chi-squared test, Student's *t*-test, Wilcoxon rank-sum test and the Mann–Whitney *U*-test, see answers to Questions 2 and 3.

Answer to Question 5

A

B, C, D and E have no statistical meaning.

Answer to Question 6

E

A, B, C and D have no statistical meaning.

Answer to Question 7

B

A type 2 error is when the null hypothesis is falsely accepted. The null hypothesis is always that there is no difference between the groups tested. An underpowered study is pointless and unethical, but does not constitute a type 1 statistical error.

Answer to Question 8

D

$p0 - p1$ is the absolute risk reduction. $p1/p0$ is the relative risk. $[p1/(1 - p1)]/[p0/(1 - p0)]$ is the odds ratio. C has no statistical meaning.

Answer to Question 9

D

Factorial trials assess two or more interventions in the same participants, thereby adding to scientific (and financial) value of a trial. Although they enable direct assessments of the interactions of the treatments being tested, factorial designs do not increase statistical power.

Answer to Question 10

B

Treatment allocation based on coin tossing (as long as it is a fair coin) should avoid biases because it excludes foreknowledge of the next treatment allocation, which might (consciously or unconsciously) affect the decision to enter a patient into a trial. Use of random number tables (either published as tables or generated by computers) achieves a similar result. In contrast, such foreknowledge is not prevented by the other methods, and those allocated one treatment by such methods may differ in a systematic way from those allocated another.

Answer to Question 11

D

Severe side effects tend to reduce medication compliance, thereby diluting the true efficacy of a drug. Conversely, interim and subgroup analyses often yield exaggerated or spurious results because they may be based on misleading subsets of the data. Non-randomised treatment studies tend to report more extreme findings than randomised studies, probably due to their inherent inability to control biases. Placebo control is needed in trials with subjective outcomes, such as pain, to avoid exaggeration of any benefit of active treatment.

Answer to Question 12

E

Multicentre trials can receive approval from regional committees to enhance their efficiency of review. The 'uncertainty principle' suggests that doctors should not enter patients into a trial if they have a strong belief in one treatment over another. The Declaration of Helsinki states that it is the right of participants to withdraw from a study at any time without providing any reason. Placebo tablets are usually used in trials where there is a degree of subjectivity, such as the self-reporting of symptoms, rather than for ethical reasons. Statistically underpowered trials are increasingly regarded as unethical because the efforts of patients (not to mention trialists) may be wasted because such trials cannot usually provide information that is capable of changing clinical behaviour (unless such trials contribute to subsequent meta-analyses).

Answer to Question 13

E

The use of a control intervention, such as standard treatment or different dosages of the same treatment, helps conceal treatment allocation and avoid certain biases. To avoid reporting a biased subset of the data, the main statistical analysis in a trial should compare the outcome among all patients originally allocated one treatment (even though some of them may not have actually received it) with outcome among all those allocated the other treatment (such intention-to-treat analyses, admittedly, tend to be conservative). Trials analysed repeatedly while they are in progress (or which are stopped prematurely) are prone to exaggeration, so it is important to have prespecified rules governing such interim analyses. Multicentre recruitment is helpful because it enables extrapolation of trial results to different settings. Collection of biological material is appropriate in some but not all trials.

Answer to Question 14

B

The exact method of randomisation does not influence statistical power, as long as proper randomisation is achieved. In contrast, the effective sample size is determined mainly by the number of clinical outcomes available for analysis, which is influenced by the number of participants recruited, the risk status of the population and the duration of follow-up. A large number of interim analyses can decrease the power of a trial by increasing the threshold needed to achieve statistical significance, because there is an increasing risk of false-positive results with each additional data exploration.

Answer to Question 15

D

Meta-analyses combine data (either published data or primary data collected from investigators) to help enhance the statistical power of trials and to explore, in greater detail than otherwise possible, reasons for potential diversity (ie heterogeneity) among study results. They may be limited by the selective publication of striking findings (ie publication bias), if such studies skew the available data.

Answer to Question 16

E

Forest plots aim to summarise trial results in a concise and accessible way, with each study represented by a row of information, its measure of effect (eg odds ratio) usually represented as a square and its confidence interval represented as horizontal lines emerging from the square. However, they do not provide a visual test for heterogeneity, which is achieved by specific statistical tests.

THE MEDICAL MASTERCLASS SERIES

Clinical Skills

CLINICAL SKILLS FOR PACES

PAIN RELIEF AND PALLIATIVE CARE

MEDICINE FOR THE ELDERLY

Haematology and Oncology

HAEMATOLOGY

Cardiology and Respiratory Medicine

CARDIOLOGY

RESPIRATORY MEDICINE

PACES Stations and Acute Scenarios 191

Gastroenterology and Hepatology

GASTROENTEROLOGY AND HEPATOLOGY

Neurology, Ophthalmology and Psychiatry

NEUROLOGY

Endocrinology

ENDOCRINOLOGY

PACES Stations and Acute Scenarios 3

Nephrology

NEPHROLOGY

Rheumatology and Clinical Immunology

RHEUMATOLOGY AND CLINICAL IMMUNOLOGY

PACES Stations and Acute Scenarios 3